H. D. (Henry Dawson) Lowry

Make believe

H. D. (Henry Dawson) Lowry

Make believe

ISBN/EAN: 9783337414085

Printed in Europe, USA, Canada, Australia, Japan

Cover: Foto ©Lupo / pixelio.de

More available books at **www.hansebooks.com**

TO PHYLLIS

CONTENTS

The Meeting	*Page* 9
The Magic Painter	22
The Lady and the Treasure	43
Green Grapes	55
The Doll's Funeral	74
When Doris was a Mermaid	91
Dreams about a Star	107
A March of Heroes	121
A London Picnic	137
A Long Journey	159

The Meeting

HE Visitor was one of the fortunate people who find a potent spur to industry in their own natural indolence. Had he attempted to apply himself he would have achieved no more than others. But he loved his leisure; he had need to earn his bread; and he had even something of a conscience. The three tendencies co-operated to give him the name of one who worked industriously, for he was habitually lazy until conscience or depleted pockets drove him to his desk. There he applied himself most

vigorously, until he had done more than was required of him, and his conscience, relenting, told him he might idle again.

A happy indisposition—the spring-time usually found him in need of a holiday—had taken him to a little western village, and for days he had idled delightfully. Then, one morning, he visited a studio where a man was working, and, remembering after a time how he himself hated interruptions when he was at his desk, he apologised for the intrusion and descended into the garden.

Doris was picking the last of the daffodils, and regarded him gravely as he approached and introduced himself.

"I know you very well, it seems to me," said the Visitor. "I've seen you so often in pictures that——"

"O!" she answered; "I'm sitting again this year, worse luck! Horrid!"

"But surely——" began the Visitor.

"It's only sixpence an hour," she continued.

The Meeting

"And that is not enough?" he asked. It occurred to him that sixpences must go far in a region so remote from shops.

"Sixpence a half-hour would do," said Doris; "sixpence an hour is not enough."

After this the conversation drifted to general subjects.

Doris wanted to know if her new acquaintance could turn cartwheels. A certain "Frank" had learned the art from his grandmother's page-boy, when on a visit to London in June. The child had not been able to acquire it yet. "And then there's spelling," she said.

"Beastly nuisance, isn't it?" responded he.

This timely interjection put the twain into complete accord with each other. "Would you like to see my garden and my bower, my treasure cave, my white rats, and my rooms?" said the lady of the garden.

"I would, indeed," was the reply, and it gave pleasure.

"That's right. I like people who like to see things!" So the two started on a tour of the garden.

The child's garden showed no particular signs of her possession of it, beyond the fact of being cleared of the docks that flourish rankly under the elders of the hedge. But the bower was delightful. You got to the top of the broad earthen hedge, and then, if you squeezed yourself through the elder branches, you might at last find a place to stand upright in. The best bower was the child's; but the visitor flattered himself he had done the right thing when he managed to get into that which belonged to Frank.

"Will he mind?" he asked.

"O," said the child, "it is mine really. I only lend it to him. You can have it for to-day, if you like."

"There's a way down to the studios, if you would care to see them," she continued. . . . . "Well, perhaps there isn't much time. But I wish you could come.

The Meeting

You see, these painters never properly empty their paint-tubes. You can't, if you don't slit them down the side and squeeze them. They don't think of that; and if you go to the dustheap you can find as many as you like. I've got lots of paint that I found in that way."

She evidently had, even if the Visitor was right in supposing her whole stock was displayed upon her face and her pinafore. He had

THE LAST OF THE DAFFODILS

interrupted her that morning in the midst of her first painting.

As for the treasure cave, it was a hole into which you might plunge your arm up to the elbow, excavated at the bottom of a heap of garden rubbish that in the course of many years had decayed to earth. It was empty; but the mouth was none the less religiously hidden from view by a mass of withered grass.

"It's a grand treasure cave!" said the Visitor.

"Then you'd like to see the treasure?" said Doris.

"Have you a real treasure?" asked the Visitor. "I used to hunt for one when I lived down in these parts; but I never found it, and in the end I grew tired and went to London. I should like awfully to see yours."

They climbed the steep garden path, stopping to glance in at the glass studio, just then empty, and at the three white rats—who were unwell, and refused to show more than the extreme tips of their tails. At last they reached a little wooden building, which was the child's sanctum.

"Come in," she said, and for a while explained the decorations of the walls, and displayed her small belongings. She produced some of the paint-tubes she had found upon the dustheap among the studios, and, slitting them down one side, proceeded to demonstrate the wastefulness of the artists who had thrown them away, incidentally adding to the display of paint upon her face and pinafore.

Then, "*This* is the treasure!" she said, displaying it suddenly.

Somehow or other, certainly not by the most diligent searching of the dustheap, she had secured a great store of gold paint. Then she had taken stones, and a small metal needle-case, a little key, and a few odd scraps of iron. Copiously gilded, the stones were now huge nuggets of solid gold, the key looked as though it might

 have been made to open Pandora's box, and the other trifles lay about them with a delightful appearance of simple preciousness.

"Where did you find them?" asked the Visitor, enviously.

"I didn't find them. I—but I will tell you my secret."

"You can trust me so early?" asked the Visitor.

She looked at him. "I can always tell at once," she said, proudly. "Well, you remember the picture you saw in the Academy last year with all the gold in it? There was a lot of it left over, and when father had finished the picture he was so tired that he said he never wanted to paint again, and that I might take the rest of the gold paint and even his favourite brushes. Afterwards he said he thought he had better keep the brushes, because he might have to work again some day, but I took the paint.

"Now, at first I did not know what to do with it: you can't paint pictures all in gold. And then Frank and the others came one afternoon, and we played in the garden. 'Let us hunt for treasure,' said Frank.

"'I should like that,' I said, but the others wanted to play a real game, for they knew the treasure would have to be make-believe. They generally do what Frank and I want them to do, but that day they would not. So at last, not thinking much, but only trying to persuade them, I said, 'You say there is no treasure. You don't know all that I know about the garden.'

"Then they all asked me what I knew about the garden, and they were quite certain that there was a treasure I could show them. I didn't know what to do, so I pretended to be angry.

"'No,' I said; 'we'll just play hide-and-seek as you wanted to. Frank and I will look for the treasure to-morrow, perhaps.' They begged me to tell them all about the treasure, but I refused; and when they went home, I asked Frank to come alone the next day. He waited for a minute after they had gone, for he was as puzzled as they were about the secret. 'I say: is there anything really?' he asked. But I would not tell him."

The Visitor interrupted. "Was there anything?" he asked.

"I expect there is," said Doris, "but I did not know of a real treasure. I could not think what to do, for I did not want to disappoint Frank. So at last I thought of a plan. Do you see this treasure? This is a key, and that is my needle-case: this used to be for hanging hats and coats on, and that is part of a lock. I gilded them all, and when I had done that I took them out into the garden and buried them. It was just down there where that tall yellow flower is growing. It is an evening primrose, and the flowers die when the sun looks on them.

"Now the next day I went and saw the Gardener, who always does what I ask. 'Lor', Miss,' he said, 'I'll do anything you mind to, but you won't find no treasure here. Why, there isn't a square foot of ground I haven't turned over every season for twenty year past. But if you're goin' to hunt for treasure, I'll dig for 'ee.'

"So I went out and found all the others. 'You can come and watch me hunt for that treasure, if you like,' I said, and they all came. It was funny, but Frank was the only one who did not believe in the treasure. 'I say, Doris,' he said, 'come over here;' and when I had stepped aside he asked me if I did really know where one was. I told him I did, and still he was not quite sure.

"'Honour bright?' he said.

"'Honour bright!' I answered; and then he pretended to the others that he had not doubted at all from the beginning.

"Well, of course I did not find the treasure at once. I made the Gardener hunt in about twenty places, and once he nearly refused because he had to dig up a cabbage. Then the children began to get tired and grumbled a little. I did not notice that, but Gardener began to think he had dug pits enough: 'I believe you'll do better to go and play one of your games,' he said. 'It don't look as if there was any treasure here.'

"I would not give up, but they grew tired. 'Very well,' I said, 'we'll just try once more, and then if we don't find anything, I will hunt by myself after you are gone.'

"So I led them to the place where I had hidden the treasure.

"'Dig there, please,' I said to Gardener; and he dug, and the treasures were turned up one after the other, like potatoes."

The Meeting

"Is that the end?" asked the Visitor, as the child paused.

"Of course not," said Doris. "They are always asking me about the treasure, and wanting to know how I knew it was there. Once or twice Frank has almost quarrelled with me, because he thought I ought to tell him. But, of course, I couldn't. You will keep my secret?"

"Indeed, I will," said the Visitor; "as many as you like to tell me."

The Magic Painter

HIS is one of the secrets Doris confided to the Visitor during the time of his sojourning down there. It need not have been a secret at all, but for the foolish incredulity of Martha, who laughed at the story when it first was told her, and was manifestly insincere when, afterwards, she professed to be convinced of its truth. Doris did not really care, knowing that the evidence she possessed made her position unassailable. But she is unaccustomed to ridicule, and so a beautiful story became a secret.

The Magic Painter

You must know, to begin with, that Doris's father is a painter, and that he delights above all things in making portraits of his daughter. Moreover, as is only natural, these pictures, giving him such great pleasure in the painting, are no whit less to the taste of those for whom he works. So Doris can hardly remember the time when she was not accustomed to sit for him.

"What a jolly dog yours is, Doris," said the Visitor one morning in the garden. "What do you call him?"

"I call him *Christmas*," said Doris.

"Did you get him given to you at Christmas?"

"Yes. At least——" Doris paused and looked at her companion rather critically. "Would you like to hear another of my secrets?"

"Of course I should," said the Visitor, and the story followed without further delay.

One Christmas Eve, Doris was sent to

bed at an unreasonably early hour. As a matter of fact, she always is; but, knowing her parents have the best intentions in the world, she usually goes quietly, after having made a merely formal protest. She did so on the occasion in question, but, having got into bed, found it more than usually difficult to get to sleep, since she was greatly troubled with many grave cares. Of course, you do, generally speaking, get pretty well what you want (if you have duly announced your wants) at Christmas-time. But it is not always so, and the things that Doris desired were so beautiful, and she desired them so much, that she was more than a little afraid she would never get them. Some, at least, she thought, would surely be missing : and her need of each was so great that she felt certain the absence of a single one would be a disappointment making imperfect her pleasure in the rest.

There had been carol-singing in the village ever since the dark evenings began,

The Magic Painter

and Doris had learned many of the Christmas songs most loved among the people. Being a-bed, she saw that to sleep would be the best way of passing the long hours that must elapse before the morning. And so, to quell distracting thoughts, she sang these carols softly to herself. Her cares still troubled her, however, and at last she bowed to the inevitable, ceased her singing and let herself think of them. Curiously enough, it was then she fell asleep. On that point she and Martha are agreed: she certainly fell asleep.

But in the middle of the night she must have arisen and wandered a long way, for when she became conscious of what was going on around her she was in a place she never had visited before. Another child might have been frightened, but the place in which she found herself was a studio, and in front of her was an artist engaged upon a half-finished portrait of herself. It was all so natural that she was hardly surprised, and before she had time to wonder how she had managed to forget the way in which she got there the artist turned on her the pleasantest face that she had ever seen.

"Getting tired?" he asked. "I sha'n't keep you more than another ten minutes."

"I'm not at all tired," said Doris. "I don't seem to have been here more than a minute."

The artist laughed softly, and Doris liked him better than ever. "Yes," he said, "I do paint quickly, don't I? But then you are a capital sitter. Had much practice?"

"Lots!" said Doris, emphatically. "I am always sitting. I——"

"You don't like sitting?"

"Yes," she answered, but in a voice that told him that her answer would have been "No," but for her desire to spare the feelings of a comparative stranger. "But I don't think sixpence an hour is enough."

"Perhaps it isn't very much," said the painter, "and you such an excellent sitter."

He began to work again, and once more the child was amazed at his rapidity. " Fond of singing ? " he asked, pleasantly, without glancing in her direction.

" I'm going to have a really good soprano one of these days," said Doris. " At present I can't sing very loudly, but that's rather lucky, for I sing to myself a good deal when they make me go to bed. I was singing to-night. . . ." She paused, for the daylight was streaming in through the skylight, and she was not very certain about the time. " I was singing last time I went to bed," she continued, " to keep myself from thinking."

" Ah," cried the painter, " you've found it a good thing for that, have you ? I find there's no plan like it. Now, if you would sing me one of your carols I should paint the quicker, and you would forget that you were sitting." Doris began to sing at once. A thing which puzzles her to this day is that the song she sang was not one of the carols that were being sung in the village. The words and the music both seemed quite new to her, although she knew them perfectly, and to this day she cannot remember where and how she learned them:

> *Lady Mary, in your bower*
> *Why weep ye sadly?*
> *Tall and white your lilies flower,*
> *All birds sing gladly.*
> *Mary, Lady Mary,*
> *What sorrow bear ye?*

> *'Tis the child that shall be born*
> *(Foolish thou, who questioneth),*
> *'Tis the crown of cruel thorn,*
> *And the sure appointed death.*

> *Mary, Mother, left alone,*
> *Why go ye gladly?*
> *Wherefore make ye not your moan,*
> *Weeping most sadly?*
> *Mary, Mother Mary,*
> *What comfort bear ye?*

The painter worked while she was singing and the child marvelled at the swiftness with which the picture progressed.

When she found that she did not remember any more of that strange new song she broke into speech. "It is almost like stepping in front of a looking-glass," she said.

"What is?" asked the painter.

"Being painted by you," said Doris, and the painter laughed again very pleasantly.

"I do work rather quickly, don't I? You see, I have such a lot to get through."

"Do you paint many pictures?" asked Doris.

"Whole galleries full," said the stranger, who by this time had become her friend. "I am at it all the time, and I paint all kinds of pictures: this sort of thing, and landscapes and castles — lovely, strong castles that never fall into ruins and never get deserted, and all sorts of things. . . . . I say, I wish you'd sing me another song."

Doris sang again, and still the artist painted. Presently he had finished. He looked almost idly at his picture while

Doris went through the last verse of her song. When it was ended he spoke:

"You see, I've finished."

Doris darted across the room and stood looking at the picture, almost as if she had really been looking into a mirror. She was

The Magic Painter 31

accustomed to be painted skilfully, but the celerity of this stranger left her absolutely amazed.

"You might almost be a photographer!" she said.

"Well," said the artist, with a little air

of embarrassment, "I suppose I am almost as quick. .... By-the-bye, Doris, is there anything you want very badly?"

"Presents?" asked Doris.

"Yes," said the artist.

"I can't tell you how many things I want, and I want them all badly. It's like a box of building bricks: if one were away the others would be of little good."

"Do you expect to get them?" asked the stranger.

"Well," said Doris, confidentially, "I don't know. I generally get what I want when Christmas comes if I have told them, and of course I have done that. But, then, I have never wanted such nice things before, or so many."

The painter began to fumble among his brushes.

"For example," he said, "what do you want most of all?"

Doris meditated.

"There's a red leather music-case," she

said. "I should like to carry it when I go to my music lessons."

"Ah," said the painter, "we will see what we can do. I don't think the picture is quite finished, after all. Suppose you sit for a few minutes longer? Do you mind?"

He found his favourite brush and began to paint into the picture such a music-case as Doris had described. She watched it growing on the canvas, and as it grew more and more like the object of her desire she began to envy her pictured self. Presently the artist finished and had turned to speak.

"Is that the sort of thing you——?"

But he had no time to complete the sentence. Doris uttered a little cry of joyful surprise.

"Look!" she cried.

By some strange piece of magic she was holding the red morocco case the artist had imaged in his picture of her. It was the very thing she had been wishing for.

"Did you put it into my hand?" she asked. "You must be a better conjurer than the one we saw last Christmas."

The artist laughed his pleasant laugh.

"But I thought that one of the things you wanted would be of no use unless you had all the others as well?"

Doris remembered. What he had said was true, but she had been so delighted with the music-case for a moment that it was a grief to be reminded of the fact.

"Yes," she said, "it is true. There was a top I saw: a top that went on spinning for ever so long, and made the loveliest sort of music all the time."

"This kind of thing?" asked the painter,

going back to his canvas. In a very few moments she began to see that he understood what she meant, for the top he painted into the picture was the exact likeness of the one she wanted.

"Yes," she cried, "that is what I mean." Then, while he added the finishing touches to the painting, she grew silent and listened. It seemed to her that she could hear, now that his painting of the humming-top was almost complete, the sound of its wonderful music. Of course she understood now that this man was a magic painter—probably a fairy, though he might have been an angel—but still the music puzzled her. And so she uttered a cry of something that was almost fright when a very beautiful top, which for some few minutes past had been spinning musically on the floor beside her, ran down, and rolled under her chair noisily.

"It's you again!" she said. "I wish you would come to my party."

"O," answered the painter. "I think

it's both of us together. But you may as well tell me the other things, mayn't you?"

"If you don't mind," said Doris, and she told him one after another what were the presents she had been desiring. One by one he added them to the portrait he had painted of her, and each, as its likeness was completed, appeared miraculously in her hand, or on her chair, or even on the floor at her side. There was quite a pile of beautiful things at last. Doris had begun to be very much delighted, and he did not need, having finished one addition to the picture, to ask her what he should paint next. She told him. But at last she had nothing to say, although it was easy to see that there was something lacking.

"Is that all, then?" asked the painter, turning with brush in hand. "It doesn't seem many."

"No," said Doris, "there is another. But——"

"But what?" demanded the painter, when she paused again.

"It's a dog, I want," she said. "I'm sure you can't do that."

"You see," said the painter, and in a few moments the loveliest long-haired Skye-terrier in the world began to appear on the canvas.

Doris was delighted. "How did you know that the dog was to be one of that kind?"

"Was it?" said the painter. "I suppose I must have guessed. You know, I'm rather good at guessing. It isn't a bad dog, is it?"

Doris did not answer. The picture of the dog was almost finished, and she was wondering how the real animal would make its appearance. The stranger painted on, making it lovelier and lovelier every moment; and suddenly there was a dog on Doris's lap, jumping up to lick her face and barking as a dog only can bark when it has found its dear mistress at last after being lost a long while. And as Doris tried to quiet it, so that she might thank the painter, she suddenly opened her eyes and found herself in bed.

How she got there she could never tell, for she had brought all her presents with her, and the dog was on her bed, barking and kissing her face as it had been doing when the painter and his studio disappeared. In a moment Doris was out of bed, and going, the dog at her side, to her father's and mother's room. Curiously enough, her father was not asleep, although the morning was full early. On the contrary he was standing half-dressed at the bedside. He turned as Doris entered. "Hullo, Doris!" he said: "Are you awake so early?" Then the dog dashed forward as if to make his acquaintance. "Why, you've got a dog!" he said. "Where have you gone wandering in the night?"

Doris did not know, and although her father described to her the personal appearance of every artist he knew of dwelling within a radius of twenty miles, he still hit on no one who bore the least resemblance to the man to whom she had been sitting. "Perhaps he's a new man," he said. "If so he's pretty sure to call round one of these days. By-the-way, did you remember to thank him?"

"Of course I did," said Doris; "but the dog was jumping up and licking my face, and before I could quiet him I found myself in my bed. But all the things he painted in the picture were there upon my bed, and the dog was still barking and licking my face. So it can't have been a dream."

"Of course not," said her father. Then his voice and his face changed together. "Why, it is Christmas Day!" he said to Doris's mother. "Where are our presents for Doris?"

The mother had been very quiet while Doris was telling her story. Even now she did not speak at once. Then, "We must get her something nice when Christmas is over and the shops are open again," she said, not attempting to explain how it was she had forgotten the day of which she had been talking but a few minutes before Doris went to bed.

Doris was almost grieved. "To think you should forget! Still, it came all right, for the painter gave me everything I wanted. I don't believe there'll be anything left for you to give me but chocolates." Then she went back to her room, and in a few minutes was telling the story to Martha, who came to dress her. Martha, as you are aware, behaved unworthily, but it really didn't matter. Her foolish incredulity only made Doris fonder of the gifts of the Magic Painter, and every one who has since been trusted with the secret of how they came to Doris has agreed that to say she dreamed the whole story would be to talk absurdly.

"You can't dream things and find them on your bed when you wake," said Doris to the Visitor.

"I'm afraid not, Doris," said the Visitor. "And yet one goes on dreaming."

The Lady and the Treasure

HE Visitor, being for the time an idle man, had taken to dropping in quite often of a morning at Doris's garden. Sometimes she laid on him the task of beguiling the hours before lunch with stories; sometimes, more greatly condescending, she would tell him her own pretty secrets, while he lounged at ease and lazily looked down upon the harbour and the quiet bay that lies beyond it.

On this particular morning Doris had demanded a tale, and he had promised obedience. But he did not desire to attempt a story, having no imagination at all, and memory only for certain private sorrows of his own. His opening was therefore an unworthy subterfuge. "Once upon a time . . . . Say, Doris, wouldn't you like to come out with me on a real hunt for buried treasure?"

"Is there any?" asked Doris, doubtfully.

"Well, if it comes to that—" he began. "But I should think we stand a very good chance. Don't you know that the Spaniards landed here long ago and burnt the place? You may depend the village folk hid their treasure when they fled; and three of them were killed. It is quite likely that to this day their plate and money lie hidden somewhere close at hand."

"But it would be no good finding it," said Doris. "We should have to give it up to Gover'ment. Gardener told me. What is Gover'ment?"

"Government?" said the Visitor. "It's you, and me, and—well, everybody else."

"Then we should get some of the treasure?"

It was the Visitor's turn to be doubtful. "Some of it, I suppose," he answered. "At any rate, we should have the fun of finding it."

Doris hesitated, deliberating. "That would be nice," she admitted. "Should we get so much as a pound?"

"At least that," said the Visitor.

"Then I think I'll come. Ellen's mother is very poor, and she wants to buy a mangle. But she's a pound short in her money, and in these hard times you can't get trust—not like you used to when Ellen's mother was young. There's so many rogues about that even honest folk must pay cash. Ellen's mother told me. I could give her the pound."

The Visitor groaned within himself, foreseeing that he would be altogether out of favour if the expedition ended fruitlessly. Yet there was nothing for it but to go

ahead. "Are you ready to start at once?" he asked.

"Quite ready," said Doris. "Now,

don't forget your pipe! Where are we going?"

That was more than the Visitor knew.

"We'll just look about until we find a likely place," he said, holding the gate open. "Or would you rather go into town and get some chocolates?"

"Chocolates!" exclaimed Doris, scornfully. Then, returning to the subject which was of importance, "Did you ever go on a treasure-hunt, really?"

"Not exactly," answered her slave. "That is: I once knew a man who did."

"You're not going to keep your promise and tell me a story?"

"It's not much of a story," he answered. "A man I know got hold somehow of a map of an island lying thousands and thousands of miles away—out there where the sun sets—with a mark on it showing where a pirate had hidden boxes and boxes of gold, silver and jewels long ago. So he got a boat and sailed away to that island—he and two or three friends. You would have seen him pass if you had been watching in your garden. Perhaps you did; but, of course, you wouldn't know."

"I remember a boat," said Doris. "It went right out towards the sunset. It was a long time ago: before you came. Perhaps that was his boat."

"Perhaps!" answered the Visitor. "At any rate, they sailed away into the West, thousands and thousands of miles. Storms came, and their boat (which was quite a small one) was often on the verge of being wrecked. But at last they came to the island, and found a quiet harbour. There was not a living soul on the island: only goats and sea-gulls."

"I love sea-gulls!" cried Doris. "I should like to be a treasure-hunter all the time."

"I don't know about that," said her companion. "I don't know that it is quite the best thing for a man. It is wiser just to be content. Mere bread-and-butter would not be interesting all the time; but one grows used to things, and one wouldn't miss it much, I suppose, if some day it were lacking. Whereas, after a week of birthday-cake. . . . . But I was forgetting my friend's story. For a whole week after reaching the island they hunted for the place that was marked with a cross on the map. Then they found it."

"And did they get the treasure?"

"Just three golden coins and a few small silver ones! Some one else had heard of the cave and got a boat and come and plundered it. These few coins had dropped out of the great boxes they carried down to their boat. My friend was very much disappointed."

"Well," said Doris, emphatically, "I should think he was. I hope that won't happen to us. Have you seen a likely place yet?"

The Visitor perceived that all the temporising in the world would be of no avail. Above the road they had been following the land rises very steeply, and in one place the hillside has been quarried. No one works there now, nor has done for many a long year. Bramble and bracken, willow-herb and yellow rag-wort fill the place, and in autumn it echoes from dawn to dusk with the voices of the children who come in companies to gather blackberries. There are also butterflies, birds, and other things, about which a man may converse, if it be necessary to talk; and in fluent conversation lay the Visitor's one hope of salvation.

"I think we might have a look at the quarry," he said. "It's just the sort of place that I should choose if I had treasure to hide."

So they walked on rapidly. Doris was so set on the quest that she did not want to talk. Her companion had his own troubles to consider and was glad of the respite. They reached the quarry and stood at the roadside looking into it curiously. It was a new place altogether to Doris, now she had realised that it might possibly be the hold of hidden treasure.

She did not for a moment observe the sudden change which had come over her companion. But presently she was aware of the silence which had fallen upon him and turned to look.

A beautiful lady was coming along the road, with the sunlight in her hair, and in her hands a great bunch of daisies dancing and swaying upon long stems. The Visitor was watching her. When she had drawn quite near he raised his hat and murmured some few words of salutation, but in such a manner that Doris had to suppose (though very much against her will) that the beautiful lady was not so nice as she appeared.

But the lady did not pass on. On the contrary, she came closer and spoke, her face all rosy. "Isn't the morning lovely? And won't you introduce me?"

The man paused for a moment, and Doris saw that he was a little embarrassed. Then, "Doris," he said, "this is Elsie. I should like you two to be friends."

The lady stooped and kissed the child. "Is it a bargain, Doris?"

Then, before Doris had had time to say how glad she would be to have it so, the Visitor spoke again. "The fact is," he said, "Doris and I had not much to do this morning, and so we thought we would come out on a treasure-hunt. The villagers, you know, must have hidden their valuables when they fled before the Spaniards all those years ago. We thought the quarry was a likely spot. What do you think? Shall we find the treasure?"

The lady hesitated. "At any rate, it's worth your while to try," she said, at last. "It is always well to try if you want a thing."

"And you will help?" said the man, eagerly.

"If Doris doesn't mind," said the lady.

So they all went into the quarry and sought vigorously for the treasure. It was rather a big quarry, and much overgrown: once or twice Doris lost them for a while, but they were always close together, and answered when she called. After a long time, during which no trace of what they sought had been discovered, Doris suggested an adjournment. "It's a big quarry," she said, "and we can't go all over it one day. And I'm sure it must be lunch-time."

The Visitor looked at his watch. "It is—nearly," he answered. "But I think we'd better search a little longer. It would be a great pity if we fared like my friend, and other people came before us and got the treasure."

"We'll hunt for five minutes longer," said Doris. "I am hungry, and they never wait for me at lunch-time."

So the three plunged once more into the innermost recesses of the quarry, seeking with renewed vigour. Doris found nothing, but presently, when the Visitor was a few yards distant from her, he uttered a sharp cry, and she came eagerly towards him through the tall bracken. "Have you found it?" she cried.

He turned upon her with a serious face.

"Doris," he said, "we should have been content with bread-and-butter. They've been before us. Look!"

The child came through the fern to his side. At his feet a golden sovereign lay on the ground.

"Why, it's like your friend's story," she cried.

"So it is," said the Visitor. "Well, it's no use searching any longer. . . . . I say: we won't say anything about this to Gover'-ment. I think it will be all right if Ellen's mother gets her mangle. You take the money."

"May I?" she cried; and then she

danced gaily along the sunny road, the Visitor on one side and the lady on the other. They would not come in to see the joy that this poor remnant of a treasure was to bring to Ellen, and when they started down the hill together Doris watched them for a while from the gate of her garden. Something about them seemed to show that they were quite absurdly happy.

"They look," said Doris, as she entered the garden, "they look as if they had really found the treasure."

Green Grapes

RE you two going out to make a call?" said Doris to her parents one day. "I am glad. There are no end of things I have forgotten to ask the Visitor this time."

The season was mid-autumn, and though the sky was of the bluest, save for a few big argosies of cloud, the blithe North-Wester that made the sea so splendid set difficulties in the way of those who desired to be idle out of doors. "I think you might play for me," said Doris when her parents had gone, "I will dance."

"What shall I play?" asked the Visitor, conscious of a repertoire whose limits were narrow.

"Why anything you like," said Doris, simply, "I can dance to any music."

"Lucky child! I believe you can." He walked across to the piano and presently began to play a waltz. The child danced around the room, serenely unconscious, and the man watched her over his shoulder, chancing on a wrong note at intervals in consequence. When this had happened Doris would glance at him laughingly, but dancing still; and sometimes she called her commands, "A little faster, please!" or, "Can you play a little slower?"

A polka followed the waltz and then a

schottische. Later the child went seriously through the steps of the *pas de quatre*, and there was a second waltz. Finally the Visitor had reached the end of his stock of remembered music. He paused:

"Go on, please!" said Doris. "You won't think that dancing tires me."

"The truth is, Doris . . . ."

"Can you play the tarantella? Here is the music."

She produced the music, and the Visitor studied it very carefully. He played a few tentative bars on the piano.

"I think I might manage this," he said. "Give me five minutes and we will see what I can do."

"O! you can do it all right. Be quick, please. . . . . Are you ready?"

The Visitor began to play, and found the music easier than he had expected, though it held his eyes and compelled him to abstain from watching the child. The rustle of her frock of soft Indian silk was all he heard whenever the tambourine was silent, for her feet fell very lightly. He went through all the movements. Then, "Faster, faster, faster, please!" cried Doris, and in a moment he turned to see her standing, flushed and triumphant, in the prettiest pose imaginable.

"You did it very well," she said. "It is easy to dance your music."

"Yours," he corrected. "You chose the measures. Now, if it had been my music . . . ."

"What is that?" asked Doris.

"O," said the Visitor, darkly. "It is a little tune that I cannot play. But I don't fancy even you could dance to it."

"I should like to try some day," said Doris. "And that reminds me, can you kick the tambourine?"

"How do you mean?" asked the Visitor.

"It is another thing that Frank learned from the page-boy in London. You hold the tambourine above your head, so— Frank used a straw-hat—and then you try to kick it. . . . . Ah! it is no use my trying." The last words came most sadly, for she had essayed the feat and failed egregiously, being of those who cannot with ease be ungraceful.

"I don't think I will try," said the Visitor, reluctantly. "You see I have reached the uninteresting stage, and it is not well to try new things then."

"But indeed you have not!" Doris protested. "You don't even take pickles at lunch. I watched: and that is the sign. . . . . Do you know, I am very much troubled about the tambourine. I cannot do it, and I want to, ever so badly. I always do want to do things I cannot do."

"But you ought to think yourself very lucky," said the Visitor. "The best things in the world are those we cannot do, and keep on desiring to do, those that we always want and can never get."

Doris was quite impolitely amazed and incredulous. "Well!" she said.

"It is the fact, I assure you," said the Visitor. "There was a man once. . . . ."

"O, if it is a story, ..." cried Doris.

"Yes, there is a story, but I don't think I will tell you about that man. He would not interest you. He always took pickles. But did you ever hear of the fox that loved the grapes because they were green?"

"They were ripe and black," said Doris, "but he called them green when he found they were not for him."

"That is one story," said the Visitor, "but in mine the fox loved the grapes because they were green. He, too, could not get them."

"It is a new story, then," said Doris. "Will you tell me?"

"Once upon a time there was a land where all the fields were vineyards. The people did nothing but grow grapes, and make them into wine, and others came from over sea, bringing corn and spices and clothing and jewels, to exchange for the wines made in that country.

Green Grapes

"Now the grapes flourished on the sunny sides of the valleys, and on the other sides (where the sun shone only when he was high in the sky, and the hoarfrost did not melt until afternoon in the winter days) there lived a great number of foxes. They loved the grapes exceedingly, and at night, when the moon shone on the empty vineyards, they had the rarest times and did much damage there. Nobody minded much, however, for the land was very fertile, and grapes so abundant that there were plenty to spare, since even the foxes must live somehow.

"Among the others there were many little foxes . . . ."

"I know," interjected Doris. "They preach sermons to children about them."

"Precisely," said the Visitor. "Well, the fox about which I want to tell you was one of the little ones. It happened on a day in spring that he was wandering alone on the hillside, when he came suddenly upon a very old fox, who was evidently half, but not all, a stranger to the valley. He saw that the old fox was not quite sure of his way, and, having a great respect and pity for the old, who cannot enjoy themselves, he spoke to him civilly, and asked if he could be of service.

"'I thank you kindly,' said the oldster. ''Tis pleasant here in the sun, and if you will let me talk for a while I shall be properly grateful. For you must know that I am a native of this hillside, come back to spend my declining days in the land where I was young. I was looking about for the old hole: it was under a great rock, by the side of which an oak-sapling grew. It should be somewhere hereabouts.'

"'It is close at hand,' said the young fox, 'and empty. But the sapling is no sapling nowadays.'

"'Indeed,' said the oldster. 'Well, I will go back to it. Strange that I should have to ask the way to the old home. Yet I must ask the favour of your guidance.'

"The young fox trotted off with his

brush bravely flying in the air, and the oldster followed slowly. 'Ah,' he said, presently. ''Tis the very place. I feel young again at the sight.' Then he tried to frolic as his companion was wont to do, and groaned at the effect of the exertion on his aged bones.

"'Ah,' he said, 'I have said good-bye to youth. But sit you down here in the sun, and I will talk to you as my father talked with me in the old days. It were a pity that the wisdom of the old should be wasted because there were no young to hear their talk and make it action.'"

Here Doris interrupted, "Say it again," she said. "I did not understand."

"The old fox meant, I suppose, that the lot of man and beast is not to know how to do things until the power to do them is gone. They have been so long in making and collecting beautiful tools that they haven't the strength to use them when they begin to try. And there are few of them that can be handed on to the young.

. . . . But I am forgetting that old fox. He sat in the sun and talked, and the young one listened on and off.

"When he was still very young the oldster had grown tired of the valley in which he had been born. For a little while he was merely discontented: he hardly knew why. Then there came a beautiful spring day ('A day like this,' he said to his companion, looking down the slope to where a small stream ran in the bed of the valley among the silver birches) and he knew what was wrong. He tried himself with a long run upon the hillside, and knew that he was strong and swift. Then he turned away from the old valley, and travelled for many days towards the unknown lands beyond.

"'There was one thing that greatly pleased me in the new land to which I came,' he said. 'There were many vineyards there also, but the grapes were all white. I was tired of the black grapes of this valley, and the white were strangely pleasant. Yet we are always desiring a change. Perhaps it was as much the thought of the black grapes I had eaten in early days as of the comfort of this old hole in which I was born, that led me in the end to leave the country. I had lost my mate, and the children she had borne me had gone away from their home—perhaps you are the son of my son's son—and so I came back.'

"Thus the old fox talked to the young, telling him many strange things that happened commonly in the far land from which he had returned. But the younger one, when at last the sun sank and he went about his own business, remembered chiefly the tale of those grapes which were ripe when they were green, and of their wonderful sweetness. There were reasons why he could not leave the valley, and, to tell the truth, he was a little bit of a coward and lacked the courage to do as the old fox had done and go away to find the sweet green grapes for himself. But he began to grow discontented from that very hour.

"Of course he grew hungry very soon, and as the moon was shining and the air soft and warm, he went with the others over to the vineyards. The grapes were particularly delicious that year, and all the others were remarking on the fact. But the fox who had heard tell of the far country found them as tasteless as dry bread, and only ate because his hunger would be appeased. 'If only they were green,' he kept saying to himself.

"He had to go on living in the valley, but from that time forward he was never quite happy. The thought of the green grapes that were ripe was to him as the tambourine is to you: only, he had not even got the tambourine. Of course there were green grapes in the early year, but they were sour, and he knew it. He was as unhappy as a fox could be."

Doris had been listening very intently. "But you said," she cried, "that it is good

to want things and be unable to get them."

"Wait a moment," rejoined the Visitor. "You have your tambourine. In the course of time the fox found his. There was a certain vineyard with a high wall around it, upon whose outer side the sun shone but little. The fox (who was grown up by this time), had become rather solitary in his habits: a man does when he is constantly thinking of something that is not of any interest to other people. He used to go alone to get his food, and one quiet afternoon he happened to pass by the wall of the vineyard.

"Suddenly his heart almost stood still. It was at a season when unripe grapes were rarer than diamonds in that country. But one of the vines that grew inside had sent a shoot up to climb over the top of the wall and hang above the road. The grapes it bore were green.

"From that time forth the lonely fox was happier than he had thought it possible

Green Grapes

to be. The wall was a high one, and he could not get at the beautiful green grapes. He could not even find a way into the vineyard and eat the other fruit of the same vine. But he did not mind eating the black ones now, for when he had taken food enough he would come along the quiet road and look at the things he had desired so long and found at last. 'They are green!' he would whisper to himself. 'Beautiful green grapes, how sweet you will be when I have thought of a plan by which to get you.'

" If the grapes had known why he came and looked at them, and how much he thought of them, I verily believe they would have fallen of their own accord. But their ignorance did not matter. The fox desired them so much, he could not doubt that they would some day be his. In the meantime he found it good to desire them.

" The good was of many kinds. The other foxes seemed to think that the only thing worth living for was food, and they were always in the unwalled vineyards, where they did much damage. It happened that the owners began to be more careful just about this time, and so a good many foxes got killed by dogs or in traps. I have heard say that some of them were even shot. Well. .... They do strange things in foreign countries. But the fox who loved the green grapes thought that eating was the least important thing in life, and so he was hardly ever in the vineyards, and escaped being killed. There were other things: I daresay you will know when you are older, how much he escaped because of those green grapes that hung over the wall of the vineyard. This was the happiest time in his life.

"The summer passed away, and the black grapes were almost all gone. His were still green, and he still visited them, and tried to think of a plan for getting them. Now, it was late in the year, and the vineyard-owners were pruning their

Green Grapes

vines. One day the green grapes fell as he was watching them: the people inside the wall had lopped off the branch which climbed. So the fox sprang forward and stood over them, thinking they must have fallen because he desired them, or that the gods to whom foxes pray had sent them to him, knowing what was in his heart. Yet, from what he said you might have fancied that he had always been certain he would some day find his hopes fulfilled.

"'Dear green grapes!' he said, 'I knew you would be mine. I have tried to win you in a hundred ways; every day I have thought of you a thousand times, and it was so before I found you. Ah! but you will be sweet!'

"Then he drew nearer still and took one of the green grapes in his mouth. The skin had hardly broken before he knew that he had been fooled by his hope: the grapes had kept their greenness all the summer only because they had been born where the sun did not shine. They would have been common black grapes otherwise. His heart was simply broken, and all his happiness gone. He dashed down the road, leaving the green grapes there to be trodden underfoot, and to this day no one knows what became of him. .... Ah, Doris, we ought to pray when we hope for a thing very much that it will never be granted us."

The Visitor paused, feeling that his story had ended very lamely, and in a moment Doris was upon him. There were tears in her eyes, and he felt himself a criminal.

"It is a hateful story," she said. "Why did you tell it me? The things we want are good, and they are better when we have them. I am sure it is not true. The fox would have gone into foreign countries if he wanted the white grapes so badly, though I do not believe the sweet black grapes would have tired him. You do not think the story is true?"

The Visitor paused, uncertain for a

Green Grapes

moment. "Of course not, Doris," he said. "It is just a silly tale some man made up, and I told it because one grows tired of true tales sometimes. As to the tambourine, it only wants a little practice. You hold it so, and then you balance yourself upon one foot. Then . . . ."

He kicked the thing above his head and handed it to the child. "You'll learn in no time," he said.

The Doll's Funeral

NCE again, on some excuse or other, the Visitor was idling in the West, and, according to ancient habit, was much in the company of Doris. But for her, indeed, he must, so long as daylight lasted, have gone without companionship altogether, for the new year had begun, and men who had been idle through the autumn and the early winter were now working with desperate industry, lest the spring shows should be thrown open to the public lacking pictures from their easels.

On a certain morning when the Visitor went over to see Doris, these others had awakened in their beds with something of the emotions that are his who oversleeps himself on a day when he has an appointment to keep, and knows at last, by the sun that shines in at his window, or—if he dwell in London—by the volume of the sound of traffic in the street below, that he has missed the opportunity. For a moment, at the time of their awaking, it appeared to them that they must somehow have lain asleep for a month or two, and that the spring, for which they had hoped to be prepared, was already upon them.

There had been weeks and weeks of frost hard enough to make all ancient natives of these temperate seaside regions search their memories through to find recollections of a season equally rigorous, and so keep the young from undue forwardness. The green of sprouting bulbs had lacked the power to pierce the hard crust of the purplish-brown earth, and not a flower was to be found in field or garden.

During the night just overpast the wind had gone into the West, and the wonder-working breath of the great sea had loosened the earth and set drops of jewelled water instead of hoarfrost on the bare branches of trees and shrubs. The blue sky overhead was dappled with light clouds, and underfoot the roads were wet and shining. The sea was purple in the distance, tinted like chrysoprase along the shores; and, because of the wind that broke the waters, the bay looked big and splendid. You might have fancied the warm wind had brought a million little birds from over the sea: so many were the singers in a world which had been dumb while the frost lay on it.

Now, the Visitor could not but feel in some degree the magic of the morning. He, too, awoke in his bed and wondered, like the others, what was the delightful arrangement for whose fulfilment he must be up and abroad immediately. For a little time the wonder lasted, and with it the

The Doll's Funeral

natural unalloyed delight in being alive on such a day.

Then he remembered divers matters that concerned himself alone, and something of the beauty of the world was gone for him. He dressed and breakfasted, and found himself whistling at intervals the tune of a sad little song whose words go thus :—

> *If green be for jealousy,*
> *Green's the robe for me:*
> *If envy go in for yellow,*
> *Yellow let it be.*
>
> *For the red robe of love*
> *With my state doth not agree;*
> *And, if I should go in nakedness,*
> *Shameful it would be.*

He was whistling the same heart-broken little air as he walked along the road above the sea, but gradually the things that lay around him took hold upon his attention, and when his goal had come in sight, he had forgotten everything except that when

Spring comes—though it be but for a flying, mischievous invasion of Winter's kingdom—a man must needs be glad. Doris was not at the gateway, though she had often condescended to await him there on mornings far less delightful. He had a long search before he found her in the glass studio, among the last fading relics of the year's chrysanthemums. Something in her attitude, and perhaps in her environment, spoke eloquently.

"Why, Doris," he said, "I believe you are almost sad."

The child turned and faced him, and he knew at once that his guess was not inaccurate. "Why?" she asked, plaintively.

"I can't tell you," he said. "Perhaps it is all these dead chrysanthemums. There is not one but is withered. Perhaps I only fancied it."

Doris paused. "You will keep a secret, if I tell you?" she said at last.

"What is one among——" began the Visitor. Then he could not help remembering his sensations when, as a child, he had whistled in church, instead of singing, during a hymn, for his sensations at the moment were identical with them. "I think you can trust me," he concluded, gravely.

"You remember the picture of the funeral?" asked Doris; and her companion recalled the fact that he had lately invaded with her a studio where some one was painting a picture that showed the funeral of a child, the small white coffin borne through the narrow streets of the village by pretty children dressed in white.

"I remember the picture," he said.

"Well, then," said Doris, "there's going to be a funeral. It is all arranged. They told me this morning. I am going away to school."

The secret now revealed to Doris had weighed upon her friend for many days, since he chanced to be in the confidence of her parents in this matter. He had found it impossible to think of her as dwelling anywhere but in that garden looking on the sea; and so the knowledge of the thing ordained for her had weighed upon him as a guilty secret. But he had lived in the world, and so to be forewarned was to be forearmed. He had prepared himself, for the child's own sake, to greet her with congratulations whenever she should come to him for comfort. "Why a funeral?" he asked. "Of course it is hard to go away. But one's home is always down here in the West, and one can come back. And it is great fun being at school—after the first few days."

He knew now that Doris was almost broken-hearted, and all pretence of cheerfulness became impossible immediately. "What is the trouble, Doris?" he asked, and at once all difficulties were over.

"I don't want to go," she said. "They say that I shall like it, but I don't want to like it. Why can't I stop here?"

"One can never stop in pleasant places," said the Visitor. "But you need not trouble, Doris: on my honour you will enjoy it after the first, and you will come back to the garden very soon."

"But it will all be different," she protested. "It will not be my garden. And then——"

She ceased again, and it was plain that she had not spoken of the situation's most tragic possibility. "And then?" echoed the Visitor.

"Sometimes you laugh at me," said Doris, "but I never mind it.... I cannot take my doll to school."

The Visitor had sympathy enough to understand. "That's the worst of growing older," he said. "One has to give up things. But you will always find something new to care for—and to give up at last. What do you mean by the funeral?"

"You remember *Christmas?*" said Doris.

She had named a dog whose history was a little out of the ordinary. The Visitor remembered at once the story to which she referred. For while the dog was still but young he had contracted a most grievous sickness. For the sake of his mistress the little creature had received more attention than many a dying child is blessed with in that village of hard-living fisher-folk. But all the care bestowed upon him had been useless, and so at last the Vet had come while Doris lay asleep and taken *Christmas* away to cure him of all pain. The child had said but little when the news was broken to her in the morning, but before the hour of lunch a new grave had appeared in the little cemetery under the elder-topped hedge (where one canary and a pair of white rats lay already), and from that day it had never lacked flowers when flowers were obtainable. The Visitor understood. "Yes," he said, "I shall never forget *Christmas*. And the doll?"

Doris showed him a limp, white bundle lying at her feet. "I spoke to the Gardener," she said, "and he has made a

The Doll's Funeral

grave next to *Christmas*. For the doll is dead. I told her what they had said to me and her heart is quite broken. Look!"

If Doris had been less like the child she was she would long since have ceased to lavish her affection on the battered thing of which she spoke. It lay supine, with eyes closed, and a dear, dead child could hardly have seemed more wonderful than did the doll to the Visitor.

"You are going to bury her?" he asked.

"I must," said Doris, plaintively. "Will you come and walk with me?"

Somehow or other the Visitor failed to be completely sympathetic.

> *For the red robe of love*
> *With my state doth not agree;*
> *And if . . . .*

He began to whistle the tune which had haunted him all the day, and then, remembering the situation, ceased disconcertedly. "Do you think I should be in the right place? I thought that only children might come in the procession?"

"They are all children in the picture," said Doris, doubtfully.

"I thought so," answered her friend. "Do you think I might be the crowd at the grave? I would like to come in somewhere."

Doris almost forgot her sorrow in her joy at this solution of the difficulty. "That will be just right," she said. "Will you go down and wait?"

She turned away and looked down upon the doll. The Visitor paused at the door of the studio, and saw her lift the veil which covered the thing's face, and look down tenderly. Then she took it in her arms and held it to her breast, lifting it very gently, lest the eyes, which were now decorously closed, should open and remind her of yesterday, when the grief of to-day was unforeseen. He noted also a box of yellowish cardboard that lay on the floor hard by, and then disdaining to

The Doll's Funeral 85

spy upon her sorrow, he went away to that part of the garden in which he knew the cemetery lay.

The garden was utterly void of flowers, and as yet no token of life had appeared above the earth. He descended the steep, grey-gravelled path, and stood beside the little pit in the wet earth. Again the little song came to him, and he whistled idly as he waited for Doris.

The gardener was working in an obscure corner. He stuck his spade into the earth and came across to the grave which he had dug at the child's request. "Have 'ee heered tell of the funeral?" he asked, in the most subdued of voices.

"I am here to help," said the Visitor. "Do you know that she is going?"

"Know it?" cried the old man. "I've known it for days, and felt worse than I can 'ee all the time, for she would come down as usual, and she was all the time talking about what she would do in the spring, when the daffodils was here again, and

The Doll's Funeral

primroses thinkin' to bloom in the hedge. I'm glad that she do know, but I can't fancy the garden with her gone out of it. What is more, I haven' got the heart to watch her funeral. I'll be gone out of sight at once, I believe."

He turned away, and the Visitor was left solitary beside the little grave.

The child came at last. She was bareheaded, and the grief in her face—though it could last but an hour or two—was not less real from the fact that she wore the pretty frock and the big useful pinafore of every-day life. She held the yellow cardboard box tightly to her breast, and the Visitor, understanding that the ceremony was very real to her, removed his hat and waited.

"Shall I be sexton too?" he said, presently; and when she did not answer he took the box from her arms. It seemed to him that she would fain have resisted, but she yielded in the end. He knelt and was about to place the box in the hole which

had been prepared for it. But Doris forgot her attitude of mute compliance with the harsh decrees of fate.

"Let me look at her once more," she cried, entreatingly.

"What is the use?" asked her companion; but none the less he knelt beside the little pit and lifted the lid of the box. The waxen creature's eyes were still closed, and he knelt regarding it until he heard a sob from Doris. Then he let the cover fall very gently and rose to his feet. "What comes next?" he asked, touching the child's hair lightly, and watching her sad face closely.

"I must say *good-bye*," said Doris. "Good-bye! Good-bye!"

"And now," he said, "shall I throw in the earth?"

"You must," said Doris; and the Visitor took a spade from the hedge-side.

The Doll's Funeral

But as he did so it was evident that some new thought had struck him. He hesitated. "You have forgotten one thing," he said.

"What is it?" asked Doris.

"There are always flowers," he said.

"But the winter has been so cold," she said; "there are no flowers in all the garden, and all the chrysanthemums are dead."

"There ought to be flowers," said the man.

"They are all dead," said Doris.

"Ah, well," said the Visitor, "that is the way of flowers. But I think I can make it all right."

He plunged his hand into his breast pocket, and produced a pocket-book, which he opened carefully. There was a moment's pause. Then he drew from the book a brown pressed flower, that might once have been a rose. He held it reverently between his fingers, hesitated, and then dropped it into the little pit.

"There," he said, "that is what was wanted."

"Thank you," said Doris, as he began to throw back the moist earth into the pit and cover up the flower and the box.

"By-the-bye," he exclaimed a moment later, as they mounted the steep, grey-gravelled path, leaving a heap of brown earth behind them; "what did you call her, Doris?"

"I used to called her Hope," answered the child.

When Doris was a Mermaid

THEY were leaning over the side of an old green-painted boat, just off a rocky island that lies not more than half a mile away from the land. It was late afternoon, and even the waves seemed to be sleepy. The water was very clear, and they could see the shifting of the brown weeds that covered the rocks at the bottom. Doris, on her part, declared that she had caught glimpses of more than one fish down there, and the Visitor was envying her good fortune and leaning over the side in the hope that he might presently come to share it.

"I like you, do you know?" said Doris. by-and-by.

"Do you, indeed?" asked her companion in tones of absolute surprise, as he sat up in the boat. "Whatever for?"

"You believe so many things," answered the child. Then, noting, perhaps, that he was still a little puzzled: "I'm sure that you would never say there are no such things as fairies."

"I should think not," said the Visitor, much relieved. "That is the sort of thing you are simply bound to believe if you want to go on living."

"But have you ever seen any?" asked Doris, forgetting all about the world beneath the waters, and facing him eagerly.

"I am not quite sure, Doris," he said. "I fancy I used to see them pretty often once upon a time. But, anyway, I don't count for anything. You may be certain plenty of other people have seen them. Have you forgotten the tale of a man who broke a fairy's leg with a stone? It is in a book."

"You never told me," said Doris, reproachfully.

"Oh, it is not very much to tell. There was once a farmer who had long wanted to catch a fairy and make it tame. He thought it would be a very nice pet, and lucky to have about the house. Now, one night he was coming home in the moonlight through a very lonely lane, and he heard little voices singing this song as they danced among the daisies just inside the gate of one of his own fields:

> *Join your hands till a ring ye make,*
> *(Dance, O dance in the moonlight!)*
> *Dawn will come if the ring ye break,*
> *While ye dance in the moonlight.*
>
> *Men will wake if the ring ye break,*
> *(Fairies, dance in the moonlight!)*
> *Haste ye, then, and your pleasure take,*
> *Dancing here in the moonlight.*

"He crept on quietly, and looked over the

hedge. There were full a hundred fairies, none of them bigger than the daisies, and all most beautifully dressed. They were dancing gaily. Now, the farmer wanted a fairy, and he was not a kind man, so he picked up a stone and flung it at the dancers. In a moment they had all gone, except one poor little chap who lay on the grass in a dead faint. The farmer had broken his leg with the stone.

"It was late, and the farmer had to be up early the next morning. He knew that no one was likely to be passing in the meantime, so he just went home to bed, and almost before daylight he went down to fetch the fairy."

"Did he find it?" asked Doris. "And

did the dawn come when he broke the fairies' ring?"

"I forget what the book said as to the dawn. As to the fairy, it is supposed his brothers rescued him," replied the Visitor. "At any rate, he was gone. But the stone that the farmer had flung at him was still there. So you see, it is clear that fairies do exist — or did when that book was written."

"I suppose it is," said Doris, accepting the logic of her friend, after a moment's reflection. "At any rate, I believe it, and so do you."

"Quite right," answered her friend. "And it need not concern us what other people say."

Doris pondered. "And what about mermaids?" she asked, presently.

"How do you mean?" replied the Visitor.

"Well, did you ever feel quite certain that once upon a time — hundreds and hundreds of years ago, perhaps — you were something different from the thing you are now?"

"That's rather puzzling, Doris," was the reply. "Yes, I have been something very different from the thing I am now. Why, not so long ago . . . . But tell me what you mean."

Doris leaned over the side of the boat, and looked down once again into the clear water. "Look down," she said, and when her comrade had obeyed, she was silent for a space, and seemed to watch the shifting of the brown weed as if it would remind her of something she had almost forgotten. The Visitor was quietly watching her, and presently he spoke:

"What were you going to tell me, Doris?"

Doris still gazed into the water with a very grave face. "Once upon a time," she said—"a long time ago, I think—I was a mermaid."

"Yes?" said the Visitor, without surprise. "How is it that you manage to remember? Most of us forget things of that kind."

"I don't seem to remember," explained the child. "But I know everything that mermaids and mermen do, just as well as I know the ways of men and women and children. And I could not know if I had not been one of them, could I?"

"I should say it was quite impossible," replied her companion, with a seriousness at least equal to her own. "But won't you tell me all these things that you know? I shall understand them better while I look down into this clear water and watch the brown weed."

"That is like my hair used to be," said Doris. "It was very long then, and it floated about my head, moving just as restlessly as the weed does, because it is never so still that there are not little movements under the water. It never troubled me, though, as it does nowadays, when the wind blows hard, for it just floated and floated like a living thing, and never came before my eyes except when I was playing with the others. Then we would chase one another under the water, and turn quickly, or suddenly dive deeper, and of course it would blind us for a moment. You got caught, sometimes, before you had begun to see again, but mostly it just floated round you and was not in the way at all. It was like the weeds down there."

She was still gazing into the clear water, and now she grew silent, forgetful of her story.

"Is there no more to tell?" asked the Visitor.

"O, there is no end to tell. Sometimes when I am sleeping I seem to go back to it all again in my dreams, and so I shall never forget."

"You may be sure of that," muttered the Visitor a shade bitterly. Then speaking to the child, "Go on with the story, won't you?"

"Let me see," said Doris, "where shall

I begin? O, there was the dancing. I suppose you would not think that you could dance down under the water? Of course we did not go right to the bottom: it was in the green water with the light coming from above, and the pale sand just showing underneath. No one could ever get tired with dancing, for the water let you move through it as a gull moves in air: you just floated and floated as I told you my hair did. But I had almost forgotten to tell you about the gulls."

"What of them?" asked the Visitor. "I suppose they would be good friends of yours?"

"Not at all," came the answer, promptly. "They hated us. Sometimes, when the surface of the water was like a ceiling of bright glass because of the moonlight, they would fall asleep on the little waves, and if we rose suddenly to find how the wind was blowing, and whether the sea would be stormy presently, we should wake and frighten them. And there were other

things we did. I don't think they were very kind," she added, reflectively, " but they were not meant to be unkind. We did not understand them. Still, the seagulls hated us.

" I used to like the clean, sandy places best of all : it was so beautiful to see the mackerel go by between you and the light as you lay there resting. The black rocks were terrible sometimes ; great crabs, and lobsters, and cray fish waited in hidden holes, and some of them could kill a mermaid easily. There was a big, dark cave, too, that none of us dared to go near. We wanted to find out what was inside, and scores of big terrible arms were always beckoning us from the opening. But once upon a time—ages and ages before—a merman had gone to find out what was in the cave, because a mermaid had told him he would not dare, and he had never come back. So we never went near the cave, though we all wanted to know what was in it, and the big terrible arms were always beckoning us to come. Of course I know well enough now what must have been in the cave: it was a big octopus. I should think the cave must be over yonder, underneath St. Michael's Mount."

She paused, and looked across to the Mount, dreamily. "But what did you do for flowers, Doris?" asked the Visitor, knowing well that even in dreams the child could not imagine a happy world that was not full of flowers.

"Flowers?" she cried. "Did you think there were no flowers down there?" Why the weed grows in forests, waving constantly, but never sighing as the trees do, because it is the moving water, and not the wind, that sets them swaying. And there were all sorts of flowers of all the colours you can fancy. I never used to pick them; they all seemed living creatures, just as much as the anemones."

"And the storms and wrecks?" suggested the Visitor.

"I don't think I remember much of the wrecks," said Doris. "There were terrible storms sometimes, and then it grew very noisy after the quiet we usually had, and so we used to go out into the deep water and find a sandy beach. There we could forget all

When Doris was a Mermaid 103

about the storm that had frightened us, though it was dark in the deep water. But there must have been wrecks, for we had golden cups to drink from and rings upon our fingers, and we used to play with gold and silver coins. And once a storm passed over and we found a little baby floating in a sort of box on the waves. We wanted to keep it, but it would have died if we had taken it down to our own place, and so we swam to the shore, dragging the box with us, and there we left it high up on the sands, giving the baby a pretty coral to play with. I wonder how we guessed that babies liked to play with corals? We watched, and presently a woman came down and walked along the tide-mark searching for something. When she found the baby she took it in her arms and was glad, so that we knew she was its mother. But presently she looked out to sea and cried, and then we knew that the baby's father was the captain of a ship which had gone down in the storm. So we went back to our own place, for we felt ashamed."

"And how did you stop being a mermaid?" asked the Visitor.

"I don't quite remember," Doris confessed. "Sometimes I seem to recollect that I went to sleep and got caught in the nets of the fishermen, and that they took me away and made me a prisoner. There was a picture of it in London. But I am not quite sure. I only know that something happened and then it was all ended. I was not a mermaid any more, and I longed and longed to go back. So, I suppose, my heart broke at last, and I died. But sometimes—even now—when I wake from dreaming I still long to go back again."

"Do you?" said the Visitor, softly.

"I go to my window and look out, and the sea is shining in the moonlight. Once I thought I heard the mermen and the mermaids singing, and always I know they are lying out there in the quiet water and looking up at the stars, with the starlight round them on the waves. And a bed is uncomfortable when you remember that."

She paused, and looked wistfully out across the waters, dotted so far as the horizon line with the brown sails of the fishing-boats which had gone creeping out while she told her tale. "One of these days," said she, softly, "I shall have learned to swim well, and I shall be stronger than I am now; then I will come down to the beach one warm night in the summer, and swim out and try to find them; I think they would be glad to see me again."

"Doris," said the Visitor, "I should very much like to come with you if you'll have my company. But I, too, must learn to swim better, for we may have a long way to go."

Dreams about a Star

HE sun had fallen behind the hills, and in the east, far away across the quietness of the sea, a big planet had come into being. They had explored the rocky island thoroughly, and, as time advanced, the Visitor gradually guided his companion back to the place where they had left the boat.

"But we won't go yet," protested Doris. "There will be small rosy clouds to look at for a long time yet, and they have only just lighted the harbour light. Let us stop here and talk for a little while."

"We are evicting the cormorants," said

the Visitor. "They sit here every evening, and they will be terribly disturbed in their minds. We had better go."

"Do you see that star out there?" said Doris, changing the subject suddenly. "I thought of a story about it the other day."

As the child had shrewdly calculated, her companion immediately arose out of the stooping posture in which he had been bending over the boat's painter. "One of your own?" he asked.

"A sort of thought that came to me!" she answered. "I will tell it you if you don't mind vexing the cormorants."

"Well, then, the cormorants must put up with a little vexation for once," said the Visitor. "Put on this big coat of mine, and I will sit and listen."

He stepped into the boat and fetched an overcoat in which Doris obediently wrapped herself. With her permission he filled a pipe and the two sat down together, just a yard or two above the gentle rise and fall of the water.

"All the stars are other worlds," said the child at last. "But that one is the most wonderful of them all. Shall I tell you about it?"

"I thought you had promised," said the Visitor, gravely.

"Well, of course you know that all the worlds were not made at the same time. God sat in His own place, and looked down upon the earth, watching it. Sometimes, when He had been thinking a long while, the people walking down here on the dark nights, when the moon was not up, would see a star appear in the sky quite suddenly, and then they knew He had made another world. Perhaps there are still new stars that come, but the sky is very full, and so I have never seen a new star come, though I have often watched. You only see when judgment day comes for one of the worlds up there, and a star falls like a wax match that you throw away."

"By-the-bye, Doris," said the Visitor,

"there's a little song that goes more or less after that fashion. It goes . . . . But I will tell you about it some other time."

As a matter of fact, he did not give it her until the morning, but you may as well receive it now :

> God made this world, and long it stood,
>   Lone betwixt moon and sun :
> Never might His first children watch
>   The stars come one by one.
>
> For the great Maker sat enthroned
>   Above this mortal strife,
> And daily pondered on the world
>   That He had called to life.
>
> And so His later children saw—
>   Wandering on moonless nights—
> The vault of Heaven grew wonderful,
>   With legions of clear lights :
>
> Till now the sky is filled with stars,
>   The children of His thought :
> The happy creatures of the Art,
>   Our human woes have taught.

"Now, the world that you see out there

across the sea," continued Doris, "is not an old one. It is one of the last that God made, and He had been thinking and thinking about making worlds for more years than there are sands on the shores of all the seas."

"I want to know about this, Doris," interrupted the Visitor. "Have you been reading, or is this just a story?"

"O," said Doris, airily, "I suppose it is 'meddling with creation,' as Father calls it. But it sounds true. I thought of it one day when I was sitting for the last picture?"

"Did you?" said the Visitor. "I knew as soon as I saw it that you must have been thinking while it was being painted."

For a moment there was silence, and the child's face took again something of the look it bears in *The Traveller*, a picture you will surely remember to have seen. It shows a young child innocently setting forth, alone and unprotected, upon a journey towards the distant horizon of a great lonely tract of country. You might fear for her, because of the unknown dangers of the journey, were it not for the courage in the serene grey eyes. With the same eyes Doris looked out towards the star as she renewed her tale.

"Every one is altogether happy up there: even the older people have plenty of pleasant things to do. You see, there must be people to do things for the children, and the old ones know that. They are all very nice, and the children simply go and ask them whatever they want to know; and they grow wiser and wiser by slow degrees, until, when it is their turn to be old, they can tell the same things to other children. So there is no need of schools."

"Do you know, Doris," said the Visitor, "there's another song, which is wonderfully like what you have been saying. We ought to be going back very soon, but it is not a very long song:

Dreams about a Star

I love my mother more than words
  Can tell, also my father;
I love my uncle, and his friends,
  But still I wonder rather

Why God compels us to be old
  Before we're tired of playing:
To sit in chairs, and talk, and still
  Say nothing worth the saying.

But I suppose He made the world,
  And put young children in it,
To pick His flowers, climb trees, and play;
  And then He saw, next minute,

There must be people tales to tell
  To children, and to feed them,
To build them houses, and to find
  Warm clothes, if they should need them.

So, children, come and play with me:
  You soon will be grown older;
And every day is as a night
  That hourly groweth colder.

And you, who once were children too,
  Be careful what you're saying,
Lest ever you should chance to speak
  A word to stop our playing."

Doris looked at him suspiciously. "Where do all your songs come from?" she demanded. "You must have read a lot of books, and you would be very useful in my star, for the children are always singing, and you could teach them new songs when they are tired of the old.

"For the only lessons they learn are pleasant ones. They learn to sing and to

Dreams about a Star

dance, and some of them learn to read, so that they may know what is in the story-books. But many of them do not trouble. You see, those who have learned to read are always glad to please the others, and proud of what they have learned. Out in the gardens—all the roads run through gardens in that star—you will see them sitting in little groups under shady trees, one reading while the others listen.

"Besides, the old people have not forgotten what it was like to be a child, and so they are just children grown bigger and wiser. They come out into the gardens constantly, and offer to tell tales, and they all believe in fairies. Indeed, they cannot help it, for the fairies have not had to go away from that world, and you see the mermaids when you are down by the sea."

"It must be a lovely world to live in," said the Visitor. "But what happens when the children are not good? For I suppose they sometimes do wrong?"

"I don't know about that," said Doris, after a moment's reflection. "You see, they are never told not to do the things that all children want to do, and you cannot do wrong when there is nothing you are told not to do. . . . . There are some things, of course, that must be punished. But I am always sorriest when I am not

Dreams about a Star

punished, and I expect it is that way with them."

The twilight was deepening, and the last traces of the rosy sunset had vanished from beyond the pines at the summit of the western land. The Visitor began to grow restless.

"Do you know," he said, "I wish we could buy this island."

"What would you do with it?" asked Doris.

"You should be Queen of the island, and I would be at the head of your servants, and then we would see if we could not start a new world that should be just like that star of yours. We would ask all the people we like, and a lot of brave men and women we have heard of but never seen; and, of course, any children who were unhappy would come to us. We would live here all the rest of our days, and grow flowers, and just be happy. Can't you imagine how we should sit here in the evenings (there would be a beautiful,

rosy, beacon light shining after dark, and steps cut in the rock), to watch for the children who would come down to the shore and take boats across? I think your gardener should have charge of the ferry. He would like that kind of work."

"I believe you will have to be the ferryman," said Doris. "You see, the gardener will be busy all the time with his flowers."

"Ah, well!" was the reply, "I shall be glad of the post if you think I could fill it properly. I shall know all your rules, at any rate, and be able to tell them to the newcomers as I take them over. But now

I must be your ferryman in quite another way; for we really must go back."

Doris looked across at the mainland, seeking for a light high up on the hillside. "I suppose we must," she said, wistfully. "And perhaps I shall be grown old before we can buy this island and begin to try your plan. But—there's a harbour over there, and steps leading up from the water. Shall we try to think that you are the ferryman you will some day be, and that this is the first day we have owned the island and we both are going over?"

She rose, and her companion held her hand as she descended the rock and stepped into the boat. He began to row very quietly, the sounds of life about the harbour growing every moment clearer and nearer. At last they had reached the steps that lead up to the quay.

"After all," he said, "this is an island, too, and if only the people knew there would be no need for us to buy one, they would set to work and make a whole world like your star. It wouldn't be so very difficult."

"I wonder if we could explain it all to them," said Doris, as she dropped the rudder lines and made ready to step out of the boat.

A March of Heroes

ORIS was blind. The folk who loved her knew that the grey eyes would some day see as well as ever they had done. But, for the present, she must live in darkness, and, since learned surgeons mostly dwell in London, she was an exile from her garden by the sea, and waited in a strange house in London until her sight should be given back to her. She and the Visitor had changed places, for it was now his part to play the guide, and this he did as one having a task set him whose performance is a joy.

The child had, fortunately, a passion for

music. The Visitor did not appear (as Doris remarked to him one afternoon) to have much work upon his hands. He was for ever coming to see her, and the tales he told were past numbering. "I believe," said Doris, on the occasion mentioned, "I believe you do nothing but walk about thinking and thinking what story you can tell me next, and that when you have found one you come straight away to tell it." As a matter of fact, she was not far from the truth. But still the flow of stories was not altogether unfailing, and there were times when the Visitor had none to tell. It was on such occasions that he remembered her fondness for music, and was grateful for its existence, After all, her affliction was but for a moment, and, in any case, it was no particular affair of his. But he had brought away with him from that holiday in the West so vivid a memory of the child among her flowers that he could not now get away from the thought of her sitting in darkness, lonely.

He had therefore a great desire to tide her over this period of evil fortune.

"I'm going to take you to a concert," he said, one evening. "Are you ready?"

Doris sprang to her feet as she might have done in the old days. Then she remembered and stood waiting until her mother came and guided her from the room. But when she returned, ready for the expedition, her cheeks were flushed and her voice full of excitement and delight. A cab came and they drove towards the concert hall.

"I wish you could see things, Doris," said the Visitor, clumsily. "We'll have good times together when you are well again."

"Yes," said Doris, wistfully, "I should like to see the houses, and the people, and the streets. But they're not all golden, are they? I used to think they were, once upon a time, when I was small."

"Not golden exactly," said the Visitor; "but they are very lovely. The horses are so strong, and tall, and swift that you'd think you must be under their feet every moment. There's a soldier going by on the pavement in a blaze of light; you should just see how he strides along, stamping his feet so that his bright spurs may jingle. And do you hear that music? Little children are dancing there by the side of the street, and the people who go by are giving them pennies. The man who plays the organ has a very bronzed face and white teeth, and he laughs when the people give their pennies, and turns the handle faster. And there are ladies going by in lovely frocks. O, it is a brave sight altogether!"

Doris sighed. "Go on," she said, "you, more than any one else, make me wish I could see; but I love you to talk, because sometimes, when you are telling me things, I almost do see. It is like dreaming."

They had reached the hall, and the Visitor helped her out of the cab and led

A March of Heroes

her by many winding passages to the seats he had engaged. In one of these passages a young man stepped in her way clumsily, and then started back and apologised very abjectly. He had seen her face, and understood why the Visitor was leading her by the hand. His voice was so full of regret that Doris (who thought her friend was never angry with any one) wondered more than a little to hear the tones in which he put aside the stranger's apologies. But within a very few moments they had taken their seats, and there was no time to ask for explanations, for her friend was telling her all about the great hall and the people in it : the lovely dresses of the ladies, the misty fountain in the centre of the floor, round which people gathered, and the huge stage, all decked with flowers and palms. He had not nearly exhausted the subject when the people began to applaud, and the music, which had ceased for a moment as they entered, began again.

It was a beautiful song, if rather sad, and the voice of the singer was clearer and sweeter than anything Doris had ever heard. She waited silently until the end was reached, and then, before the applause had died away, she turned to her friend. "Tell me about it," she said.

"I told you about the flowers and the palms," he said. "Well, you look away over them and there's an old garden, with a young moon shining beyond a dark hedge, and a few stars out. There's a lonely tower in the garden, and at the topmost window a beautiful lady."

"I know her," whispered Doris.

"The lady is looking down into the garden and she would like to go down, but I don't think the people in the tower will ever let her. There's a man in the garden looking up at her window, and he knows that she will never come down, nor he get up to her, and yet he cannot help hoping. I think the hardest part of it for him is that he is not at all certain that she would come down if she could: whether there is really anything could keep her in the tower if she wished to come down to the garden. So he stands down there and sings to her, and the lady listens."

"Always?" asked Doris.

"Yes," said the Visitor, "I suppose it will be for always."

Then the singer came back and began another song.

"Tell me about it," said Doris, softly.

"They seem to be all sad songs to-night," he answered. "The garden is gone and it is a great lonely place where very few people ever come. A little girl, who has never in her life had a friend, or heard a voice speak kindly, is wandering there alone. She is tired and hungry and very much afraid, and if it were not that she feared the wild beasts which live in the desert she would lie down on the hard ground and go to sleep. And now the man is singing to her, and she is afraid."

"What man?" said Doris.

"A tall man with a pale face that is almost terrible, until you look closer and see how kind the eyes are. He is telling her not to be afraid of him."

"And the little tired girl?" asked Doris.

"She is still afraid of him: he is so tall, and his cloak is black, and his face seems hard and stern because she cannot see his kind eyes for the darkness. But he goes on singing and I think she is beginning to know he is her friend. Yes, she has run towards him now, and he has taken her in his arms. He is still singing, but much more softly. Listen."

"She is falling asleep," said Doris. "What is there more?"

A stir began among the orchestra and the audience applauded once more. "That is the end. I can see nothing now but a concert platform, with many lights and flowers and big palms. But here's the music again. We must listen."

The programme called it a Cavalry March and added a wealth of miscellaneous information for the benefit of those who cared to read. Many young men were reading it to the ladies who sat with them. But the Visitor simply waited until the music had lasted for a few moments and then bent down and talked to Doris.

"Can't you tell what it is?" he asked.

"Tell me," she said, and he began his tale.

"The Queen is there in a gold crown

and a dress all diamonds and rubies, sitting on a throne that blazes with gold and jewels like the sea at sunset. And all the men who ever have fought for her go by on horseback. Can't you hear the fall of the hoofs, and the clash of swords and harness? .... These are the young men who go by first. They have fought and won the victory and they are proud of it. Some of them have wounds, perhaps, but they quite forget them, and their sweethearts stand looking on, and wave their hands as they march on and on. And the Queen sits and watches them go by, and is proud, because they are all her soldiers .... But listen! Can't you hear the cheering a long way off? The sweethearts and the mothers of the soldiers are not looking at the men who march by. There is some one coming who is a very great man, indeed, and they are all waiting till he comes. The music gets louder and louder: how those trumpets ring out!

The people are cheering and waving their hands. Ah! there he is at last. Isn't the music splendid?"

The music had suddenly grown louder; the instruments of brass crashed insolently.

"Who is he?" asked Doris, breathlessly.

"He's an old, old man in a curious hat with feathers in it. His head is bent forward a little and his lips are tightly closed. He has grey hair and his nose is rather big."

"It's the Duke of Wellington!" cried Doris.

"Of course! I knew I'd seen his picture somewhere. He looks very stern and like a real captain, because men go out to die quite gladly if he tells them to do so. But now he looks up at the Queen and he takes off his hat. His head is bent lower than ever, and you can see that he would do more for her than all these men would do for him. The Queen is proud because he is her servant, and so he marches on.

"Do you notice that the music is changed? The mothers and sweethearts have gone, but the Queen still watches. These are all old men. The first one looks as though he would have hardly strength enough to walk if you took him off the horse, and the man beside him has lost an arm, and the empty sleeve is pinned across his chest. But when they come to where the Queen sits watching, they do not feel old any longer, and they are just as proud as the young men were just now."

The music changed.

"The Queen is proud of these men, too, but they go by without looking up at her, and I fancy they think she is ashamed of them. Their swords are broken and some have lost their helmets. Some are wounded and have bandages round their heads, and they all look tired and broken-hearted. You see, they went out to fight the Queen's enemies and they were beaten—there were not many of them, and they had to march through a country where they had little food and where they fell sick of the fever. So the Queen's enemies triumphed and these men were beaten. A lot of other men—some of those who passed by just now—went out and fought with better luck, and the Queen's enemies were driven into the desert and never troubled her again. These men have gone sadly with bent heads ever since, because they let themselves be beaten; but if only they would look up they'd see that the Queen is as proud of them as of the others, because they did their best; and that she loves them a little better because it was their luck to be beaten."

"Why don't they look up?" asked Doris. "But the music is changing. Who is coming now?"

"'There's such a crowd that I can hardly tell you. The streets are full; at every window there are people waving handkerchiefs, and even the housetops are crowded. The soldiers go by more quickly, and, though the crowd hides a good deal, I can see their plumes and feathers, and I know that they are closer packed. And that— I don't think I need to tell you, for you can hear the fife and drum. But a regiment of boys is going by, quite lost in the crowd. Yet the Queen can see them, and they, too, make her proud. They've gone by now, and the plumes and feathers pass as they did before. They hurry past, for they all want to get a look at the Queen, and now——. Why, they've all gone by, and there's only a concert platform, decorated with flowers and green palms."

The music ceased, and presently this march of heroes was followed by other music. Doris listened for a while, but it was plain she was no longer interested.

A March of Heroes

Presently the Visitor suggested that they had better be going, and she was manifestly well pleased. He had never known her to be impatient of her blindness until to-night, but it was easy to see, as he led her through the crowded corridors, that it irked her greatly now. She was eager to get to the cab, and having reached it, she leaned back in her corner with a little sigh of contentment. The man, conscious of an evening successfully filled, followed her example and lit a cigarette.

In the gentlest way imaginable Doris expostulated. "Don't, please!" she said. "You'll make me cough, and I do so want to think about your soldiers."

The man apologised and flung his cigarette away. Presently, when they stood upon the doorstep, Doris repeated something she had often said before: "There's no one makes me long to see as you do. And yet——"

"Don't you trouble, Doris," said the

Make-Believe

Visitor. "You'll see clearly enough one of these days."

And Doris wondered, for it seemed to her he spoke almost sadly of the granting of the gift for which she was praying day and night.

A London Picnic

HERE had been talk of a journey up the river to celebrate the return of Doris to the sunlight she loved so well. But when the day of her delivery arrived the Visitor was wakened early by the noise of rain against his window, and a glance at the low grey sky told him the expedition must inevitably be postponed. For the child's sake, to whom sunlight and shadow had been the same for many long days, he was exceeding disappointed, and vainly racked his brain for subtle consolations.

But Doris was well content. "Even common things, like the rain, and the grey houses, and the people who go by, are pleasant to see again," she said, as she sat at the window looking out into the desolate London street. "And the flowers you brought are wonderful. When I've grown tired of the common things, it will be fine again and we can go upon the river. Then I shall have enjoyed both."

So the two sat together and looked at the rain, talking of many things. The afternoon passed pleasantly enough, but the Visitor, vaguely conscious that he ought to find some substitute for the expedition which had been postponed, was not altogether happy. Suddenly he had an idea.

"You've never seen my rooms, have you?" he said.

"No," said Doris. "You promised to ask me to tea."

"Come this afternoon," said the Visitor. "Run along and get permission and then put on your cloak and hat. Be quick: we'll have to go marketing first."

In five minutes they were in a cab once

more, and another five brought them to the most wonderful shop in London, its window lovelier with many-coloured sweets than any garden with flowers in the spring. The cabman waited in the rain while they entered. "You must do the ordering," said the Visitor. "My part is to pay."

Doris brought sugared violets and rose-leaves, and beautiful biscuits and cakes. "I think that is enough," she said presently, and they drove to a place where strawberries were to be had. At last they reached the lofty building that was the Visitor's abode, and mounted to the fifth floor chambers whose windows looked upon a desolate world of cloud and windy chimneys. The Visitor sought his housekeeper. When he returned Doris pointed to the pictures that were so numerous as almost to conceal his wall-paper.

"What are these?" she asked.

"They are pictures of Japan," he answered, speaking with a shade of reserve in his voice, for his Japanese colour-prints kept him chronically upon the verge of bankruptcy, and excited the derision of many excellent persons among his friends.

"Tell me about them," said the lady.

"There isn't much to tell," replied the Visitor. "They are just pictures of Japan. That man with the sword, who stands among the sedges, is an actor; that pink one is just some girls going out for a holiday and taking turns to ride on a black horse. Here is a lady, caught in the snow, and this one has been out in the rain and got wet: see, she is wringing the water out of her dress."

"And this one?" asked Doris.

She pointed to a lovely triptych whose acquirement had been a piece of extravagance only justified by the improvement that was effected when it replaced a Tottenham-Court-Road overmantel which had been in the chambers when the Visitor first entered into possession.

"Oh," he said, "that is a picnic in the springtime. All those girls have gone into the country for a time, and they are sitting under the cherry blossom. See, one of them is so happy that she has written a little song about the Spring, and hung the paper on the branches so that the birds may learn it. They have pretty names in Japan; this one may be Miss Blossom, and that Miss Butterfly: they will all have names like the names of fairies." He paused, seeing the child's face.

"What a pity that we also could not have a picnic!"

"Yes!" said Doris.

"I wish . . . ." began the Visitor. "Do you know, the Artist has a place just over the way. You'll like him. We will go and have a picnic over there. It will be quite Japanese, for he never has any room left on his table and spreads his cloth on the floor."

Doris did not answer. The Visitor spoke a word with his housekeeper. They passed down a long passage, and then the Visitor knocked at a door and opened it. "This," he said, addressing a young man who came forward, "is Doris."

"I'm delighted to see her," said the Artist.

He took some books, drawings, pipes, and things from an old high-backed chair, beautifully carved. "Will you take this chair?"

Doris moved across to the chair, and for a space surveyed the great untidy room in silence. There were a few paintings, mostly unfinished, but the majority of the pictures on the walls were drawings in black and white. She did not attempt to investigate them closely, but even so she perceived they had stories attaching to them, and that these stories must needs be fairy-tales.

"Where is the table-cloth?" asked the Visitor. "All the other things are coming: rose-leaves and sugared violets, strawberries and very thin bread-and-butter—all the necessities of life. The fact is, Doris and I were to have picnicked up the river to-day, and as the rain prevented that, we came here, and invite you to join us."

The cloth was laid. The tea came, and Doris was waited on with care.

"I see," said the Visitor, presently, "that you are looking at the Artist's pictures. Now, the Artist has more secrets than any man you ever heard of. His experiences would make a whole bookshelf full of fairy-tales, if only he would tell them. But he never will. Ask him about the City Beautiful and the Wonderful Bird. He won't tell you."

"Please do!" pleaded the child, regarding her new acquaintance.

"I'd be very pleased," said the Artist, looking most unhappy, "but——"

"You see, I was right," interrupted the Visitor. Then, turning to the Artist, "At least you'll show her the pictures."

The Artist produced some drawings, and Doris looked at them with grave, interested face. Most of them showed a city such as you may see sometimes when the sun sets

in a sky full of broken cloud. But it was evidently a real city, and you could tell the Artist must have known it well who could draw it in so many aspects and yet compel you to recognise that it was always the same city he was depicting. As to the bird, it was a monstrous creature, terrifying of aspect, albeit the pictures showed it for ever engaged in the performance of some useful task, whose object was usually the pleasing of the children of the City Beautiful.

"Do you know the story?" said Doris, appealing to the Visitor as the last drawing was inspected.

"I suppose I could tell it," was the answer. "The Artist won't."

"I should be most happy——" began the Artist.

"I shall have to tell you myself," said the Visitor, and as he settled to his task, the Artist and the child were equally intent upon the narrative, as if it were new to both.

"Down in the worst part of London, where no flowers could live, even if the people knew there were such things and cared to plant them, there lived a man called Jim Smith. He was wicked, dirty, and stupid, and I don't remember anything about him that is good. But he was the owner of the bird.

"The fact is, he hated honest work, and used to get his living by all sorts of irregular methods. In the spring he sold watercresses, and of course he had to go into the country to get them. Early one morning he was coming back to the railway station with a full basket on his back. There were birds singing and flowers everywhere—you remember how beautiful it was last spring—but he did not notice any of these things. He merely wanted to get back to London and sell his cresses, and spend the money wickedly and stupidly.

"But presently something caught his eye. It was a big cobweb, and there were

A London Picnic

great shining drops of dew on it. The man saw that it was beautiful, and beautiful things always vexed him. He raised his stick and did away with the cobweb. Then he went on his way feeling a little happier. He caught his train to London, sold his cresses, spent the money in drink, and found himself at the police-station at night. The next morning the magistrate ordered him to be kept there for seven days."

Doris interrupted. "But where are the Bird and the City?" she asked.

"I was wondering myself," said the Artist, handing her the rose-leaves. "And it's my own bird, too."

"We shall come to that in time," said the Visitor. "In fact, we have come to it now. Doris knows well enough that we do not see the fairies nowadays because they have grown smaller and smaller ever since Christ came. Well, a very tiny fairy indeed, and a prince in his own country, had been caught in the spider's web that Jim Smith destroyed because it was beautiful;

and he would have been eaten by the spider if the stick had not fallen at that very moment. He was extremely grateful, and filled with a desire to do something for his benefactor. Not having a plan ready, he followed Jim into London, saw that he lived in a very terrible region, and, late in the day, beheld him carried into a place whither he strongly objected to be taken, and lodged in a cell that had not even a proper share of daylight. He went back to the fairies and called a council, for he was resolved to liberate the man to whom he owed not only liberty, but life itself. Curiously enough, the place in which the man lived seemed to him not more wretched than the prison cell. He was not accustomed to London.

"Now, the wonderful bird was the servant of the fairies. You have seen the pictures, and, but for them, I would not attempt to describe him. But he was"—turning to the Artist—"how high?"

"About twenty feet with neck coiled, I

think," said the bird's master. "I have never measured him with neck erect: I couldn't get up."

Once more the Visitor turned to Doris. He began a sentence and then paused. "You'll have to get through these sweets," he said, passing them. "Well, the bird is marvellously big and strong, but doves are not more gentle. It flies almost as swiftly as the daylight, and if ever you should see it overhead you would take it for a sparrow, it always keeps so high above the earth. The fairies met and decided to send the bird to fetch away to the City Beautiful the man who had helped their prince. The city is not theirs exactly —grown men and women, and any number of human children live there—but every one who reaches it does so because they have helped him thither.

"It is a very beautiful city, and nothing that is bad can find a place in it. No rain falls, no hail, and no snow, but a gentle dew comes in the night, and the season is always spring, because the things that fade (if there be any) are hidden from sight by new flowers opening, and new leaves that unfold themselves. It was to this place that Jim Smith was to be taken on the back of the great bird. It was given a message to him, for the fairies could not think that the man who had so helped their prince would be unable to understand the bird's talk. To children it seems like their own language, and most of the people one likes find it easy enough if ever they have the luck to get the bird sent to them. It is perfectly plain to the Artist here, and you would understand it better than you understand me."

Doris had heard too many fairy tales to take a new one very seriously. But she was careful not to emphasise the fact that she knew this was no plain chronicle that she was hearing. If only her eyes had not sparkled you might have fancied she took the whole for Gospel. "Go on," she said politely.

"Well, the man was released from prison at the end of seven days, and on the next morning went into the country to gather cresses. I need not tell you that, inasmuch as all his stock-in-trade had to be stolen, he had gone into a very lonely region. He was picking hurriedly when suddenly he began to hear a very curious noise. It grew louder and louder, and presently something came between him and the sun. The noise was the whistling of gigantic wings, and as the man looked up, he saw the wonderful bird alighting on the ground hard by. It had come to take him away to the City Beautiful where great honour would be done him. But the man did not understand. On the contrary, as the bird began to move towards him he retreated into the bed of cresses until the water was right above his knees."

He turned to the Artist: "I believe the bird is rather terrible to look at for the first time?"

Doris had listened with an occasional

"Yes?" for interjection. She also turned now to the Artist, and awaited his reply.

"Oh, if you go by appearances alone, the bird may frighten you a bit. But his manners are magnificent, and his voice——"

"Yes, his voice!" interrupted the Visitor. "His voice is charming, and if you can understand his message it is exceedingly pleasant to hear, for he has many tales to tell of the city out of which he comes. But, unfortunately, Jim Smith could not understand. However, he could not stop in the water all day—for the owner of the cresses might come, and he would be no more merciful than the bird was likely to be—so he sought dry land, keeping his eyes upon the bird.

"This is what the bird said: *Why did you stop in the water? The fairies, grateful for the delivery of their brother from death and shame, have sent me to convey you to the City Beautiful, where a palace is made ready.*"

A London Picnic

"And the man said: *Seems as if 'e was trying to talk. 'E's balmy on the crumpet, s'elp me Bob.*"

"What is that?" interrupted the child.

"Oh, he meant that the bird had not all his senses: and was balmy on the crumpet."

"Ah!" said Doris, "I shall remember."

"I wouldn't if I were you," said the Visitor. "However, the bird went on trying to explain itself. Once he stooped and showed the man the comfortable place on his shoulders where passengers were made at home on their way to the city. And the final result was that Jim Smith saw the bird was very fond of him, and believed it was a sort of harmless idiot. He tried running into the next field. The bird followed him. "If I could get him to London," he said, "there'd be a penny show as 'ud draw all Walworth." He trudged on, and the bird still followed, though it explained now and again (if only Jim could have understood) that time was getting on, and delay dangerous.

"To make a long story short, they reached the southern outskirts of London late in the afternoon. The man tethered the magic bird to a big pine-tree in a wood, and lay down to sleep. After dark he woke and led the bird into the City. The bird began not to like the look of things, but he had been sent to get Jim Smith, and a sense of duty made him follow the cress-seller until he found himself locked up in a small and dirty stable somewhere near the Walworth Road, which is the part of London where Jim Smith lived. He was left there in solitude all the night, and suffered much discomfort from the narrowness of his quarters.

"He was glad when Jim came in the morning, supposing that the business which had prevented his taking advantage of the fairies' invitation was now done. But Jim merely pitched some Indian corn—which was not the bird's natural food—into the manger, and waited. The bird was hungry and tried to eat the corn. While his back was turned, Jim produced a big pair of scissors and clipped his wing. ''E's safe now,' he said. 'An income for life!'

"You can imagine how heartbroken the bird was, now that he could not possibly expect to fulfil the duty laid upon him. He only blamed himself, who had failed to make the mortal understand his message, but his spirit seemed broken, and when the people paid their pennies and came to see him, they were amazed at the gentleness of a creature so terror-striking in aspect. This went on for a week, and Jim Smith grew prosperous, while the bird became thinner and more miserable every day on his diet of Indian corn. Then at last—— But this is not my part of the tale. You must ask the Artist for the rest."

The Artist began promptly.

"I was wandering in the Walworth Road," he said, "when my attention was attracted by a crowd that was leaving a stable. A man in a red jersey was showing the people out and asking questions.

"Some great, strong, bare-headed girls came first, to each of whom he put the question, 'Satisfied, my dear?'

"'Yuss!' said they.

"Small boys were all 'Tommy' to him, and were questioned.

"Then a stout woman in a big white apron and faded bonnet struggled up the stairs, and drew in a great breath of the air, laden with the odour of fried fish and boiling oil from a shop next door. 'Satisfied, mother?' said the showman. 'Yuss, my dear, and more than satisfied.'

"'Thank you, mother.'

"I paid my penny and entered, and somehow the bird (which was very dejected at first) perceived that I could understand his language, and told me what the Visitor has told you. Now I had lately sold a drawing to a publisher and I was rich. I bought the bird and took it home, waiting until night had come and the streets were empty. I keep it in the garden there, and it has told me many things at different times. All those drawings, for instance, are done from his descriptions of the city."

"And his wings?" asked Doris.

"The new feathers are coming at last, but the bird is almost afraid to go back, having been so long away. However, he wants me to get to the city, and so he will probably be braver when the time comes to start. Would you care to come with us—with me and the Visitor? There's room for us all on the bird's back, for I shall have no luggage beyond a sketch-book and some pencils."

Doris hesitated. "I should like to see the city," she said, at last. "But I don't think I can come. There's my garden down by the sea, and all the things in it that belong to me: for a long time—since my eyes were bad—I have not seen them. And there's the quarry where the blackberries grow, and the little island in the water. No, I don't think I can come with you."

The Artist looked disappointed, but the

Visitor appeared to think that she had decided rightly.

"You see," he explained to the Artist, "Doris has a rather wonderful garden down in the West, and a little island where the mermaids sing in the moonlight, and a quarry where there is a great treasure hidden somewhere, so that, one way and another, she is as happy down there as if she had got to the city. And she is accustomed to the garden: which is always a great thing."

"Still," said Doris, consolingly. "I'm sorry I can't come with you."

A Long Journey

HE Visitor was going a long journey into foreign parts, and there was only one thing certain: that for several years, at least, he must remain in exile. He had fortunately a brief holiday allowed him, and went into the West country as soon as he was able, taking up his abode in the old white-walled cottage above the village by the sea. It was close upon Easter-time and the spring was at its height. The country quiet was dearer than it ever had been, for the joy of being back was deepened by the knowledge that very soon this privilege of return

would be denied him. He gave himself up to enjoyment of the present, bidding those hold their peace who knew of his imminent departure.

Doris had returned to the house in the garden after her first experience of school, and he was rejoiced to find her altogether unchanged. There were things she knew, which had not yet been revealed to her at the time when they two buried Hope together. But the knowledge had not changed her: she was still Doris. The Visitor had feared that he might find her vastly aged and altered, but her twelfth birthday came while he was still in the village, and the little gift he had found for her occasioned such a demonstration of delight as proved her still the child he had known, and inspired a vague hope that Doris might be the creature so often dreamed of—the child who never grows older.

Perhaps it was this foolish hope that led him to take a little of the beauty from a day which had opened perfectly for her. At any rate, it was on her birthday he chose to tell her.

They were in the garden again, and Doris had been showing him her daffodils, which had opened under the shadow of the hedge, long after their brothers in the sunlight had bloomed and withered.

"Do you know, Doris, I am going away soon?" said the Visitor.

"O," said Doris, "I was wondering when you would tell me that."

"But——"

"You always do go away soon. But, then, you always come back."

"Yes," said the Visitor, "I suppose I shall come back. But I am going a long way, across the sea there, to a country so far off, that if you were here of a morning in your garden and wanted me, and if you called me and I could hear, it would be deep night by the time your voice reached me. I am going to the other side of the world."

Doris did not answer for a moment.

Then she spoke very softly, not looking in his direction:

"For a long time?"

"I'm afraid so?" he answered, gravely.

"You won't come back to work when the summer is over, as the others do?" asked Doris, thinking of the artists, her friends.

"I'm afraid not," he said. "I shall have to stop out there and work. More than one summer will go by before I see you again: I shall be quite an old man. But I must send you a gold nugget one of these days, and some precious stones for rings and brooches, if I can find them, for I want you to remember me."

"I shall remember," said Doris, resolutely. "But you must not stay too long, or you will be changed. I shall want to know you at once, even though all the others think you are a stranger, and your own dog barks at you when you get to your home. Come back before you are old."

"I will come back as soon as I am able," answered the Visitor. "And you will remember me, all right. There are so many things that only we two know: I will shout out some secret word at once, and you will know it is I. But.... Do you think you will be here then?.... We all have such long journeys to go, and journeys tell on people."

"I don't understand," said Doris, reproachfully.

"If only I had time," said the Visitor, "I could tell you all sorts of stories. It is curious that I sometimes had none to tell. .... You will promise to be here when I come back?"

"Of course," said Doris.

"Then I will tell you a little story: Once upon a time there was a man who wanted to be a king. He was only a gardener really, and on Saturdays he used to cut his biggest cabbages and his finest flowers (except a few, that were so beautiful he could not let any one else have them) and take them to market. So he made a little money.

"He loved to be a gardener but for some strange reason he wanted to be a king, too, and he was always trying to find a kingdom. I think he would have done rather well, even if they had put him on the throne of England, for he seems to have thought that a proper king is really a sort of servant to his subjects. And he was not particular either: he would have been quite contented if he could have found a kingdom with only one person—and himself—in it. He only wanted to be a king.

"Of course he went on searching vainly. Sometimes he thought he had found his kingdom, but he never did. He was just a gardener really, and the people laughed when they heard of what he desired. 'If it comes to that,' said the blacksmith one day, 'why should not every one be a king, and make a kingdom for himself in his own back yard?'"

"It is like my treasure!" exclaimed Doris, as she listened.

"Isn't it?" said the Visitor. "Well, the blacksmith gave the gardener an idea. 'I will make myself a kingdom,' he said to himself, 'I will be a king of flowers and plants!'"

"So he just stopped his search and went away to his garden. Now that he had disappeared the people wondered what had become of him, for he kept within the walls of the garden (which were very high) and set about the making of his kingdom. But first of all he had a new lock put on the big green gate, so that no one should enter.

"After this he never troubled about wandering outside the garden. The people missed him a little, for he had gone about doing many kind things, just to show them what a fine king he would make. I fancy he might have found a kingdom out there now, if he had still cared to try. But he had given up hoping, and the blacksmith's speech seemed to him the only wise thing he had ever heard. So the people never caught a sight of him, and when they passed by the locked gate they did not guess that he was within.

"If you had lived in Fairyland, or come on the piskies' gardens that grow on the cliffs, but may only be seen at night, you would be able to guess something of what that garden was like when the man had been working for a year or two. I don't know how it was, but somehow there was always sunlight there (or so it seemed), even when the world outside was cold, and wet, and miserable, and had not a flower in it. And, in the hot summer months, when the fields were parched, and the wayside blooms all slack and wilted, there were dews in the morning and dews at night, so that the flowers over which the gardener was king never felt weary of the sunshine, but were always fresh as the others only are at dawn.

"They were the loveliest flowers that

grew on earth. You see, the gardener gave his whole life to them, and thought of nothing else. Early in the morning he was among them, and when it was dark he sat at the door, smelling their sweetness, and thinking of what he should do for them in the morning. I think I have guessed one secret of why his garden was so wonderful. He never gathered the blooms. The buds came, and swelled, and opened, and when their time was come they dropped and mingled with the earth. And so, in the course of time, there was not an ounce of earth in all the garden which had not once been lovely blossom.

"You can fancy that the seeds planted in such a soil brought forth flowers the likes of which were never seen before. The primrose was still a primrose—or it would have been spoiled—but it had something of all the beautiful dead blooms out of which it was made. And there were scentless things—asters, hollyhocks, and things like that—which seemed to have the loveliest fragrance, because they had grown where roses had fallen and died.

"The gardener never picked a flower, but, of course, he would have no weeds in his garden. The walls had been made specially high to keep the flying seeds from entering. Only, I must tell you, he had very curious ideas, this gardener. Some things that most people called weeds he loved and cultivated because they were beautiful; and, never having been cared for until now, the flowers that were called weeds grew lovelier every day. Also, there were some things the world calls flowers and cultivates with care, that he thought weeds because they were ugly."

Doris interrupted, "Did he grow dandelions?" she asked. "Gardener calls them weeds, but I love them."

"I'm sure he must have grown dandelions, Doris," said the Visitor. "I should think you and he would have felt almost the same about most things. It is a pity that you never met him."

A Long Journey

"Is he dead?" asked Doris.

"It is just a story," answered the Visitor.

"And not a true one? I was hoping you would take me to see the garden and the man that was king in it."

"O, it is true enough," said the Visitor. "But all the true stories happened a long, long time ago; and you will hear about the garden."

He paused for a moment; then, "After a time the gardener had to go abroad."

"Ah!" sighed Doris, heavily.

"It was a great trouble to him at first,"

continued the Visitor. "He did not want to leave the garden at all, for he had made it just what he wished it to be, and he was afraid that it would change. Things do change, you know, by merely growing, and he was more and more unwilling to go as he looked on his wonderful flowers that grew on either side of the grey gravelled paths. By-the-bye, I should have told you that his garden looked on the sea, just as this one does, and so to live in it was like watching the road by which he was presently to go away.

"He did not want to go, but there was no choice left him. So he looked at the high walls he had built, and at the gate which had so strong a lock. 'After all,' he said, 'the walls are high, and the gate is strong. Nothing much can happen to my garden, and if there are changes I will soon make everything as it is now when I escape from abroad.'

"So one night he packed up his bag and slung it over his shoulders. Then he

A Long Journey

shut the windows of his house and locked the door, and went and stood at the top of the slope, looking down on his flowers that were sleeping in the moonlight. Then he moved away to the gate and opened it. 'Goodbye!' he said, 'Goodbye! I will come back!'"

"And he did come back?" asked Doris softly.

"Not for a long time," answered the Visitor. "All sorts of things happen to people who go abroad. Once a hungry lion jumped upon him out of the forest, and he would have died, had it not been for a trusty friend who was hard by with a rifle. As it was, he lay ill a long time, and when he grew better his face was terribly scarred, and he walked lame. More than once he had fever, for the air was not like the air of his garden, and then it used to seem to him at moments that if only he could sleep soundly he would never want to go back. All sorts of things happen to people who go abroad. Once he went walking in a beautiful green meadow, such as he had seen at home in the old days, and there he trod on a snake that bit him. He did not die, but for a long time afterwards he had something wrong with him and did not know weeds from flowers. And then there was his work: he had to do it, but often he felt he would never get to the end of it. Indeed, there was only one thing that kept hope alive in him: he had the key of the garden, which he always carried.

"At last he came to the end of his labours, and went down to the coast and took a ship for England. He reached London and took the train from Paddington (did I tell you his garden was down this way?), and when he had come to the end of his journeyings, he passed through the villages and towns to his garden.

"It was very early in the morning, and he sang for joy as he thought of his kingdom of flowers and how lovely it would be looking:

"*O, have you seen my garden in the West,
    And have you seen my roses red and white:
The garden I have made, therein to rest,
    The roses blowing all for my delight?*

"*O, come you to my garden, come away,
    And gather all my roses, an you will.
Leave but the buds to flower another day,
    And, O, my heartsease, prithee do not kill.*

"Now, while he was still singing, he came to a high wall, with a great green gate in it. His voice failed him, and he fumbled in his pocket for the key. Perhaps the joy of being back again had made his hand unsteady. At any rate, he could not get the key into the lock. He tried a long time, and he looked at the lock; it was all choked with dust and rustiness, and he saw that he could not expect to open it.

"So he went to the other side of the road, and looked at the wall, to see if he could climb it. Alas! he had built it so tall and strong that now it was to keep him out.

"He began to be afraid. He flung the key away and then rushed at the gate, butting it with his shoulder. The lock had been very strong, but it was now old and rusty, and at last it broke. The gate opened, and the man stepped inside. He just gave one look, and then, forgetting to close the gate which had always been kept locked, he sat down on a great block of white spar, and wept."

"Why?" asked

Doris. "Had some one got into his garden while he was away?"

"The wall and the gate had kept every one out," said the Visitor. "He wept because the garden had changed so utterly, simply by growing. He knew well enough that he himself had been altered a little by the events of his long journey. But his flowers had just gone on growing, and the garden was more changed than he. A beautiful rose-tree was grown into a great tangle of thorny branches, and the roses were all draggled with hanging to the earth. A shrub that once had been very lovely had grown bigger and bigger until it had overgrown and killed all the flowers where there had been a wonderful bed of heartsease in the days that he remembered. The daffodils that used to grow all along the front of the house were stifled under the creeper, which had become so heavy that it could no longer cling to the wall. It was all very pretty, in its way, but his garden was gone, and he had not the heart to change it back to its old beauty by dint of long labour. All the time that he had been in foreign parts, you see, he had been thinking of the garden that he left. Time had utterly changed it, and he could not care for it any longer.

"So at last, when the morning was still young, he shouldered his knapsack once more and went away from the garden leaving the gate still open. I am told that after he had gone the villagers came and entered the garden. They trimmed and pruned the shrubs, and in the end it became a very nice garden. But it was never what it had been in his time."

Doris had long had a dim suspicion of allegory, to which she gave characteristically naïve expression: "Is there a moral?"

"I don't think so, Doris, said the Visitor, " only . . . I am going away in a day or two."

"I suppose you must," answered the child, sadly. "Well, if you think this

A Long Journey 177

garden will be changed you are quite wrong. But you must be careful to come back just when my daffodils are flowering, and then you will find me here."

"Ah!" said the Visitor, "then it is not so bad to go upon that journey."

www.ingramcontent.com/pod-product-compliance
Lightning Source LLC
Chambersburg PA
CBHW022111160426

43197CB00009B/984